FIND YOUR VOICE, SAVE YOUR LIFE 4:

TRANSCENDENT MEN, REAL STORIES

Find Your Voice, Save Your Life 4
Transcendent Men, Real Stories

Dianna Leeder

©Copyright 2022 Dianna Leeder

Published by Brave Healer Productions

Paperback ISBN: 978-1-954047-62-4
eBook ISBN: 978-1-954047-63-1

CRAVE MORE
>> LIFE

Are you ready to live out loud?
Join the Crave More Life community
at
http://www.cravemorelife.com
Free gifts, tips and
elevation through finding your voice.

DISCLAIMER

This book brings together self-written, personal accounts of men's transcendence offering hope and opportunity for awareness and healing. While you may indeed find the accounts therapeutic as you read them, this book is not intended to replace professional or therapeutic help of any kind.

Know that the experts on these pages have shared their experiences and knowledge with you with a sincere intent to assist you on your own path of transcendence. Please contact them for further assistance with questions you may have on what has been shared here. Bios are placed after each chapter.

An important note: Some chapters contain content that may trigger your own abuse, neglect, or experiences of violence. If you need support, reach out to your closest mental health service. If you or someone you know is in immediate danger, call 911.

Who are you that screams,
I am to be this or that?
Beloved enough.

Haiku and cover art by author Guy Kilchrist

DEDICATION

Shall we dance, dear shadow?
As it is only through moving together
with vulnerability and acceptance,
that we shall heal and transcend.

This book is dedicated to our fathers, many whom saw life only through the wounds they and their ancestors suffered and carried, doing their best within a self-limiting social construct. We are grateful for eyes that can now see the rich, whole lives men can have as they learn to embrace the raw vulnerability that is part of each of them, part of all humanity.

To the courage and unwavering commitment of our amazing authors. The words you have shared in this book are brave and have challenged the traditional image of the male species. You have opened up your lives and used your voices to express to other men that they too, can heal and transcend to a life of freedom to be who they are called to be. You are leaders, you are guides, and you are needed in a chaotic world where the term masculinity is ripe for redefinition.

To the expansive and wide open heart of R. Scott Holmes, without whom the intention of this book would not have been nearly as rich or meaningful. He shares himself and his many superpowers with the world through the simple lens of love, and has taken up the cause of improving men's relationships with themselves and with others through accepting the needs of their own hearts.

Thank you, thank you, thank you.
The world is that much closer to true balance, within us and outside of us.

AS TRANSCENDENT MEN, WE RISE...

…to live beyond the normal,

to surpass the limits,

to move beyond a human experience,

to a shift in focus from selfishness and egoism to the needs of others,

to a shift in values; no longer driven by external rewards and demands, knowing the reward is the activity itself,

to an increase in moral concern; an intensive focus on doing what's right,

to an elevation of emotions; awe, ecstasy, amazement, feeling uplifted and of high vibration,

to being part of a movement to heal ourselves so the world can heal; bringing our strength to affect positive change for the greater whole,

to an intimate combining of aspects of the Divine Masculine with the Divine Feminine; capturing the pure essence of joyful union of the mind and the heart,

to seeking and experiencing full alignment to self; unapologetically leading with the heart and self-honour,

to having found one's voice.

TABLE OF CONTENTS

INTRODUCTION | i

A MESSAGE TO MEN
LOOKING FOR TRANSCENDENCE | vi

CHAPTER 1

AN ACCIDENTAL BUDDHIST | 1

THE JOURNEY TO FIND MY HEART

By R. Scott Holmes

CHAPTER 2

RECOVERING THOU | 10

THE GRACE IN AGING, THE SACRED SELF

By Guy Kilchrist

CHAPTER 3

REDEFINING HAROLD | 19

SEARCHING FOR TRUTH, IDENTITY, AND REDEMPTION

By James Kealiipiilani Kawainui, Native Hawaiian Healer, Mentor, Kahu

---

CHAPTER 4

HEALING THE FATHER ARCHETYPE | 28
RECLAIMING VITALITY AND SUCCESS

By Dan Gorbunow, AMT

CHAPTER 5

BECOMING THE MAN
MY CHILDREN WOULD WANT TO KNOW | 38
By Jere Friedman, J.D., M.A., CMMI

CHAPTER 6

SEEKING THE PIECES TO BE A WHOLE MAN | 47
JOURNEY TO SOUL PURPOSE

By Rev Will Halm, Reiki Master

CHAPTER 7

UNMASK YOUR SOUL | 54
FIND PEACE WITHIN

By Saahil Mehta

CHAPTER 8

MISSISSIPPI MUD | 63
A LESSON IN DISCERNMENT

By Ken Shepardson

CHAPTER 9

FINDING MY CENTER OF CALMNESS | 70
PERSONAL POWER TO THINK, GROW AND LEAD
By DK Warinner, Founder, Center of Calmness®

CHAPTER 10

SCREAMING TO BE SEEN | 79
FORGIVENESS OF SELF THROUGH HONESTY AND ACCEPTANCE
By Kenny DesChamp, B.Mus. B.Ed.

CHAPTER 11

CALLED TO ACCEPTANCE | 88
THE GIFT OF SHATTERED BELIEFS
By Matt Segebartt

CHAPTER 12

YOU *CAN* HEAL | 95
A CLEAR PATH TO DITCHING THE WEIGHT OF OBLIGATION
By Rev. Tomás Garza

CHAPTER 13

THE SACRED CARPET | 103
ON-RAMP TO A PATH OF TRANSCENDENCE
By David D McLeod, DD, PhD, Certified Master Life Coach

CHAPTER 14

REAWAKENING LOVE | 113
A VOICE IN THE LIGHT
By Patrick S. Fisher, Spiritual Coach

CHAPTER 15

WHEN YOUR SOUL CALLS | 121
FOLLOWING THE THREAD TO YOUR LIFE'S PURPOSE
By Mark J. Platten, MBA

CHAPTER 16

EMBRACING THE NOW | 131
RELEASING "SHOULDS" TO REALIZE UNLIMITED POSSIBILITY
By Shervin Hojat, Ph.D.

CHAPTER 17

ONE SIMPLE VOICE | 140
TEACHINGS FROM A SHATTERED HEART
By Joseph Uveges, Singer/Songwriter

CHAPTER 18

FROM DRUG ADDICT TO SOUND HEALER | 149
A JOURNEY OF TRANSFORMATION
By Kelvin Young

CHAPTER 19

CYCLING TO A NEW YOU | 156

DISCOVERING WHO YOU ARE ONE MILE AT A TIME

By Scott Bell, Certified Transformational Coach

CHAPTER 20

I DON'T KNOW HOW TO LIVE | 164

LIFE IS A JOURNEY, NOT A DESTINATION

By Gene Wright, RYT® 500, Certified Recovery Coach

CHAPTER 21

THERE IS NO SUCH THING AS A HEALTHY EGO | 171

STEP OUT OF THE ILLUSION AND WAKE UP!

By Patrick Dague

CHAPTER 22

SURRENDER AND EXHALE | 181

THE POWER OF SAYING NO

By Walid Aboulnaga

MEDITATION TO BALANCE THE DIVINE FEMININE
AND MASCULINE ENERGIES | 190

A LAST MESSAGE TO READERS | 194

WHOLE-HEARTED THANKS | 196

ABOUT DIANNA LEEDER | 199

INTRODUCTION

I wanted more of him.

Looking up into the night sky, I watched the snowflakes softly coming down on us, each flake different from the others, a gift of nature that was so clear through the light above the door. I wiggled on the homemade stool, crafted from a log of a fallen tree taken from the woods behind the house. I wanted to get the best view of the gracefully falling snow as I possibly could.

I could have been inside, curled up by the burning fire, watching a movie that was not too young for my older siblings but not too old for us younger ones, waiting patiently for the popcorn bowl to reach me. But I chose to pull on my red rubber boots and my jacket and head outside to be with my dad.

It was calm outside, there was no need to share space with my sisters or tolerate the incessant teasing of my older brother. Sitting outside on that damp log, all I had to do was watch the snowflakes fall and wait for some kind of recognition from my dad that I was there. That recognition was not forthcoming, he was busy building a new step for the doorway.

It's not like I expected him to stop what he was doing and play with me, but even at the young age of seven, I needed him to connect with me as more than just a figure head in the family. *I want you to know that you matter too.* He didn't know that, at least not from me. I couldn't articulate it and he was too busy scratching off the list of jobs to be done to listen, one coming off as two more were added. Even if miraculously the list had been cleared, my time with him would eventually run out when my mom called me in for bed.

My dad was a full time police officer but it was hard to support his wife and five kids, me being the youngest, on a single salary. He drove a taxi, was a security guard, and worked in construction. Other times, he would start a business and work for himself. He was a jack of all trades, skilled at any kind of labour, doing whatever he had to do to take care of us.

He lived an honourable life. He did what he had been taught to do and became who he was taught to be. Follow the rules. Provide for your family. Take care of your aging parents. Be faithful and loving to your wife. Show up on time and do the job you're paid to do. Don't abuse alcohol. Always be truthful and honest. Love your children. Discipline without emotion.

Honourable, right? Men have been celebrated for far less.

But he was also busy and distant, cool in that fall sweater kind of way, where you long for summer's warmth but you know it's evasive. In his world of little to no displays of emotional connection, there were no books read on his knee, no help with our homework, and only the occasional tucking in when my mother was unavailable. There was no giggling over silly things, no compassionate words for mistakes he or we made, no messages in birthday cards that weren't in my mom's handwriting. Even when a holiday or vacation lent itself to a closer connection among us, there was never room for expressions of what was considered the unmanly.

He was an ethical man with strong values. If he were still with us today, he would say he wouldn't live any other way. I would say that he didn't need to live without ethics and values, he simply needed to give himself permission to be whole.

His heart got left out of the equation. As a child I never saw him cry, put his needs before ours, or express his intimate feelings. He was the only one, other than perhaps my mother behind closed doors, who knew what lay silenced inside him that he wouldn't allow to see the light of day. The magnitude of the richness that could have been part of his daily existence has never been lost on me. I see it and I feel it, even today.

I heard the stories of his upbringing that I eventually understood to be one that didn't celebrate the softer emotions of a boy or a man. I watched him raise my brother in much the same way, not demonstratively denying him his emotions or feelings, just never encouraging or celebrating them.

I was outside that evening and so many others, watching the snowflakes while my dad built a new step, because I needed more of him. Even at a young age, I wanted to know him in a much deeper way, to connect with him on a level that he simply never allowed himself to show. I wanted him to be free of whatever was holding him back from being true to himself and expressing exactly who that was with whatever emotion that came with it.

I didn't get to fully know or see my dad until many years later when he was a senior and I was a parent myself. By then, the chains of social influence had fallen away, leaving him free to make choices that served him and not just others. There was no employer to demand things of him that required doing the right thing when the right thing ignored his own needs. He no longer had a family to raise based on emotionless respect and obedience, he could simply enjoy his children, his grandchildren, his great grandchildren, his traveling, and his brandy. The expectations of him as a man had changed with age.

And there was no longer a wife. The grief of loss cracked him open like a dead branch falling from a tree, forcing him to connect with his own emotion each time he saw the pillow still in place on her side of the bed, or the empty passenger seat of the RV.

Grief took him alone on the road in that RV, contemplation brought him back to his church and his deep reverence for Jesus. He wanted to be part of a spiritual community as he had been as a boy, with a relationship with God and a reunion with my mother. His spiritual connection gave him joy and ignited a spark of love and respect for himself, his family and the greater good. He was spiritually home again.

He came back to us in a softer, more loving and available way. A beautiful way that was the foundation of a loving, family relationship now based on deep human connections. He saw his own wholeness and no longer had a reason to withhold. He cried with me when the emotion was upon him, sharing the truth of his feelings for my mother and his family. He wanted to know more about me and my purpose, and the words "I love you" crossed his lips often. He spoke the sensitive truths that were his feelings with a gentle vulnerability that only comes from having permission to see, know and be himself without filters.

The walls had come down for my dad without ceremony, softly and gently like those snow flakes. I knew and understood him better in his last ten years of life than I ever had. He stood beside me and my family as himself, stripped down of any reason not to be, and my heart was happy to be witness. In the end, I got what I wanted. And so did he.

The journey of a transcended man isn't an easy one. As you'll read in these chapters, it can be filled with human conditioning that simply doesn't serve him, offering events that are traumatic and even barbaric, overflowing his life like a forgotten tap that soon damages more than where it immediately leaks. Man suffers and all his relationships suffer; parents, partners and children. Healing can't happen until the shadows, his wounds, are danced with.

Ultimately, transcendence for a man is finding his voice; healing his wounds, discovering who he is and his soul's purpose, and aligning to his own truth. With that level of self-ownership and authenticity, he has the freedom to elevate or rise up to connect to new meanings of life. The silencing by others is gone, the self-silencing of himself is gone, and the essence of the true self is invited to emerge. The whole self is engaged.

And that whole self is able to express all parts of him. The calls for strength as well as the calls for vulnerability, the soft and the strong, the yin and the yang where one gives rise to the other. The balancing of the Divine Masculine and the Divine Feminine that allow him to integrate those traits that gender has historically separated, healing our relationship with each.

When he is in search of more of what serves and feeds his true self, he's open and willing to look at ways he can live his life that truly honour him and those around him. There is discernment between the ego and the heart and the need for traditional power-over is gone, replaced with an understanding of serving the greater good.

He is saying, "I am who I am and will be all of who I am."

These are the stories of men who have faced the wounds, done the work, and are now showing up in service to their relationships and to the world.

Men, my hope is for you to write your own story, one that sees you rise as these authors have, in true alignment to self, balanced and connected in all ways, and using your voice to be more.

Women, you have the opportunity to see men differently, accept their vulnerability as the new normal, and reap the benefits of men who are showing up as whole selves. This is not us waiting solely for men to change, true change will happen when we too, show up whole. Let's support and celebrate men doing this work and intentionally take up space that is currently filled with gender stereotypes alone. Together, we can change the face of relationships.

Gentle is not weak, gentle is strong.

Having the courage to be something that life doesn't expect of you is strong.

Opening up yourself to your heart is strong.

I am honoured to present this book to the world.

Because when we share of our deepest selves, we touch the lives of others and transcend a little more.

With deep gratitude and love

Dianna xo

Dianna Leeder's own path of un-silencing herself has become the journey through which she coaches others and certifies Find Your Voice Healers. She holds the power of each of us to heal and live our purpose by aligning to self as sacred and honourable. From clients to her own grand babes, Dianna's message is simple.

"Look inside."

Find Dianna's full bio on page 199.

A MESSAGE TO MEN LOOKING FOR TRANSCENDENCE

Who we are as men really wasn't determined by us.

The way we grew up, where we lived, our family's values, the movies we watched, the jokes that where told, all hold clues to how we should show up as men in our lives.

"Always use your head. Don't make decisions through emotions. Be strong."

That's where things stop connecting for us. We stop connecting to our inner selves and our voices become quiet. It's where the roadblocks show up, where we question our ability to have the life we truly want, chasing after things that serve everyone else but not us.

No matter what gets us there, know this.
We always have ourselves to come back to.
This book is meant for you, the man looking for more.

It had two working subtitles; Modeling Masculinity with Integrity and How to be a Guy without Being an Asshole. How many of us have had no model, a bad model or the wrong model of how a man should show up in this world? For me it was to get up and go to work each day, work extra on the weekends, then rinse and repeat. Try to get one to two weeks vacation a year with the family, and an occasional night out. Life was always tied to family, home and duty, and that's all good until we ignore the need for roses and champagne too.

Where do we find true joy when battling through each day, dragging the baggage and the shadow self around with us that we acquired while young, adding to it with each small trauma at a time?

It's not until we move outside ourselves, seek another way to view us, that true change and true healing occurs. For me it was the loss of my daughter and then my wife that left me wondering if there was more. Please, don't allow major life events to be the impetus for change.

In healing old wounds, clearing blocked energy, and committing to create and sustain daily rituals, you can heal. Rituals are habits where you are present in the moment, and through them you can peel back all the layers of living that didn't serve you or who you were meant to be. In finding yourself, you are able to show up in this world as a healed, whole, compassionate man to all those you love. That's where true change happens.

Read the stories these incredible, amazing men share. You will find some awe-inspiring life accounts. Most of all you will feel what life is like through the words these men share from intimate, vulnerable and pivotal points in their lives. Your will find grace and you will find dignity. You will find reflections of yourself and your neighbours, co-workers, and teammates. And through those, you will find your own stories.

Absorb the experiences of all the writers and decide how each one might help you create more awareness of the path to your best self. What's offered on these pages are tools that I invite you to pick up as you would a hammer you've had around the house for a long time, with familiarity and confidence.

Life changing things can happen for us when we're being true to every part of ourselves. We experience what we need to, when we need to, and all that's left is for us is to give ourselves permission to make choices that serve us and our purpose.

Maybe picking up this book is the synchronicity that you are on the right path. Go there with joy, self-determination, and wholehearted love for yourself. I promise you won't be disappointed.

Transcendence is our birthright, and strong voices get us there.

Find your voice, save your life.

R. Scott Holmes

Join my Facebook group Find Your Voice, Transcendent Men. It's for authors of this book and any other man who's willing to share and learn more about himself. It's there you can share your story too.

Find Scott's full bio at the end of Chapter 1, page 9.

CHAPTER 1

AN ACCIDENTAL BUDDHIST

THE JOURNEY TO FIND MY HEART

R. Scott Holmes

How did I come to be standing in a Burmese Buddhist Temple in Penang, Malaysia? This is what mystics and yogis do. Not some blue-collar 60-year-old from Brockton, Massachusetts. Not some grandfather, father, widow, son, brother, uncle, cousin I ever knew would do something as crazy as this. On the word of a medium channeling guides I can't even see? Was I nuts to travel 9000 miles to find parts of my soul? Incredible! Ludicrous! Unbelievable! Nothing in my upbringing prepared me for this.

Gangly ten-year-old arms held the blue ribbon I just won for reciting all the books in the old testament in the basement of our small Methodist church. Sundays were Sunday school and then singing in the choir for the hour and a half service. All my cousins, uncles, and aunts attended as well. Sundays were family, food, and bonding—getting dressed up in my maroon suit coat that always felt way too tight. It was about those polished dress shoes that somehow never quite fit. Learning the bible stories and being able to retell them was important, though I didn't know why. This is what was expected of the oldest of four—duty, setting the example, fitting in.

Before settling in Massachusetts, I was an Air Force brat living in off-base housing in seven places around the world before turning eight. Movement, change and knowing your role in our growing family were the only constants. Mom held everything together while Dad did his duty.

Learning to make friends fast and to adapt were the keys to survival. Curiosity and taking everything in around me was how I dealt with that constant change.

When we moved into the house my parents would live in for 55 years, it was like walking into a dream. My room was actually going to be my room, without a little brother in it! Privacy. A place to keep my stuff and the same bed to sleep in for years to come. A backyard. Friends I wouldn't have to say goodbye to. Stability. A welcome change to my first years on this planet.

Treehouses, baseball, football, playing tag, wiffle ball, kickball, Monopoly, Stratego, Hot Wheels—growing up in the 60s and 70s in our close-knit neighborhood of Irish, Swedish, Spanish, and Yankee (another name for so many generations in New England with so many cultural influences no one really had another identity) was idyllic. Even though there were four kids under one roof, we always had plenty, and plenty was enough. Grandparents and cousins and the corner store were only a bike ride away. Walking to elementary school, junior high then high school with our friends each day cemented lifelong friendships.

Playing football, basketball, and baseball created competition and bonding among the 13 boys within three years of age growing up in our three-block community. Brockton was a small city with a rich history and provided a wonderful backdrop to the life we explored each day growing up.

Graduating high school and starting our local state college to teach History were somehow sidetracked when I met Moira. We grew up not more than two blocks away, knew all the same people, and went to the same schools, yet never met until one night—a house party became a party of two. We instantly bonded, and over the next six months, we were never apart. Elton John's "Your Song" played as we sat outside her parent's house, not quite knowing how to say goodbye. "Have you ever felt like this before?" "Never," I replied, settling my arms tighter around her, hoping love would always be like this.

Serious became immediate when through choking gasps, she told me she was pregnant. All my upbringing came to the forefront: *Love conquers all. Marry, work hard, buy a house, and create a safe life in our neighborhood where our family could grow.* I was 19 and had all the confidence that I had the answers to all the questions life would throw at me.

Five years later, we had three daughters in an apartment not far from our families. Sundays at Catholic Mass, and I was working three jobs so Moira could raise the kids, just like we had seen our parents perform. At 25, I realized I didn't even know what the questions were, forget what the answers could be. Survival, never taking a day off, and wanting more for us steeled my will, building walls and creating armor to wear into the battle each day. We found a rhythm to our lives, strained as it was.

Then the day our lives changed forever: Moira called me at work, "Something is wrong with Amanda, she woke up from her nap, and she won't respond to us." Our 15-month-old daughter was in a zombie-like state. My wife and neighbor could not get her to respond to any stimuli. "Meet me at the pediatrician's office, I'm calling right now."

Rushing into the overflowing waiting room, I walked over to where Amanda was being cradled by Moira. There was a slight twitch in the corner of Amanda's mouth. I immediately picked her up, alerting the staff she was starting to seize. Within five minutes, both doctors on duty and the nurse were doing what they could to calm down a grand mal seizure in a child with no symptoms or history of any disorder.

"We are sending her to Floating Hospital in Boston," Dr. Hourigan said. I looked at Moira's wide fear filled eyes and knew our little girl was in real trouble. The ambulance ride into Boston at rush hour, the hours of waiting and not knowing what was going on. For the first time, hearing our perfectly happy, healthy daughter wailing was devastating.

Thus began a 14-year struggle to maintain sanity, quality of life for our multiply-handicapped youngest, but also our older two daughters, paying the rent and keeping our family together. The armor I wore grew thicker as I slogged through each day not knowing how it would end.

The phone ringing at two in the morning is never good. "Mr. Holmes, I don't know any other way to say this, but Amanda has passed." Dozens of times we rushed to the hospital expecting the worst after getting a call from the pediatric nursing home that took care of her. Each time Amanda would rally. Without fanfare or an ambulance ride and medics working on her as they had so many times before, Amanda stopped breathing quietly in the middle of the night with no warning.

How do you survive losing your daughter? How can I comfort my wife or my girls from this loss? How do you fill a hole that big?

Life was supposed to be happily ever after. That's what every movie, story, and song has told me all my life. Why does life have to be such a struggle? How can this get any worse?

Be careful what questions you ask of the universe. You may not like the answers.

"This feels funny on the side of my breast." Moira was getting dressed and noticed the lump. Fifteen years earlier, her mom had passed from cervical cancer and those images and fears of the torment chemotherapy caused her mother came rushing back. *God no, don't let this be happening to her! Haven't we had enough?*

What started as a lumpectomy turned into a mastectomy then chemotherapy. And five years out, almost to the day, a recurrence of the breast cancer. Chemotherapy followed by radiation, an FDA study, more chemo, daily pills, blood tests, MRIs, CAT scans, early morning trips into Boston, late-night pain pills—all of this as she taught elementary school full time, got our daughters through college, early 20 wanderings, weddings, and grandchildren. She showed strength beyond measure, mixed with humor and always family.

I always tried to save my family, unfurling my cape and flying to the rescue no matter what was needed. I could not fix my wife's cancer. No matter how many trips to the hospital or how many different medications were prescribed, I could not cure her. *God, why do you make her suffer? I can't bear to see her in such pain. I will gladly take her place. She doesn't deserve this.*

I was powerless to change anything that happened. I felt I failed as a husband, the protector, and the hero. I could only watch and provide comfort. Where was the God I had prayed to, grown-up worshipping, trying to understand?

"Dad, you need to come down here quick; I think Mom's dying!" Struggling to get dressed from interrupted sleep and stumbling down the stairs to our make-shift hospice room, I found Moira gasping for breath after not eating or drinking for ten days, lying unconscious downstairs in a rented hospital bed. I kept the promise Moira and I made to one another to stay home and not go to a hospital. My daughter and I took turns keeping watch through the night, wondering how long a body could possibly sustain itself without nourishment. Ragged gasps were followed by that final shudder, and she was gone. Moira continued to live life on her terms, even in death.

Life took two of those I loved most in this world. I couldn't feel anymore. Was the God I had learned to pray to responsible? How could I look to Him for healing?

The wake and funeral were a blur of tears, heartbreak, condolences, and kind words, all failing to reach my heart. A week-long trip to England with my two daughters to see their best friend and her month-old child didn't bring us any closer as we were all suffering. The stop in Dublin on the way home was a way to pay homage to their mom, as she always wanted to visit her grandparents' homeland. We scattered Moira's ashes at the Cliffs of Mohr with what seemed a constant gale-force wind off the water. As I looked back one last time as we left, a rainbow appeared where we were standing. "Does that happen often?" The attendant replied, "Only dozens of times a day." I then knew we had picked the perfect spot.

Showing up to work daily, trying to make sense of my new situation, and not knowing when emotions would overtake me was disorienting. Days went by with fewer friends reaching out. My daughters had lives and families of their own. The cat had very little to say about the subject when asked. An empty house can be a refuge, or it can become a cave to hibernate in. Being single was never a consideration before. My parents were in their eighties and still living independently. Wasn't that how life was supposed to play out?

I took up yoga when I turned 50 and started making old man noises just getting off the couch. While I loved my father, I did not want to become him at such an early age. Daily morning yoga became my refuge, settling me into the day and helping me feel grounded. Listening to my body with intention allowed me to start to feel again. Feelings coming up were observed rather than overwhelming. An understanding, a tiny seed, started growing inside as I realized this was my time to find the me I always envisioned. I had the time. Now find the drive to work at it!

Paul was the best man at my wedding and retired from work as most of us know it when he was 30, although he generally worked 17 hours a day on his projects. I was turning 60 and was just going through the motions. "Let's take that trip around the world like we always talked about," reminding me of the hours we talked about traveling when we were young. Six months later, we were traveling through central Europe in an Audi SUV, making up the trip as we went along. 17 days, eight countries, dozens of churches, cathedrals, and castles, 2500 miles driven, and memories to last a lifetime. On the flight home, Paul asked, "So, where are we going next year?" Our lifelong friendship was stronger and any lapses during the last 30 years faded.

One year later, we were on a 17-day guided group travel through Thailand, Cambodia, and the length of Vietnam. Gold covered temples in Bangkok highlighted the magnificence of the Buddhist religion. In the hall of the Golden Buddha, I was overcome by the power emanating from the two-foot-tall Buddha figure 30 feet away. Its welcoming vibrations coursed through my body. Little did I realize I held our group up for almost an hour as I stood transfixed, head bowed to this powerful deity. Throughout our travels in Southeast Asia I was struck by the practices of everyday people honoring the monks, temples, their ancestors, and the meditations I observed. They seemed to walk with their God within them. Buddha was about enlightenment, understanding, acceptance, and unconditional love—transcending our everyday existence. I felt like I had come home to a place I had never been.

Still on a high after getting home from the trip, Samaha, a medium I worked with regularly, stopped in the middle of her reading and started conversing with one of my spiritual guides. "Tell him he needs to go to Penang to the Burmese Temple!" Samaha replied, "I don't know what that means." "Tell him to go collect those parts of his soul left behind." He then walked off without explanation. She shrugged and said she didn't understand any of that. Well, if she didn't, how the hell could I?

We googled "Penang" and "Burmese Temple." Sure enough, there was only one such temple in Penang, Malaysia. Also, there is a theory that soul parts get left behind when there is violence or a tragic, sudden death. They seek refuge in a place of safety. All great to know, but what could I do about all of this?

Two weeks later, an email was sent by the tour group company Paul and I used. Out of curiosity I looked up their trip to Singapore and Malaysia. Sure enough, the last stop on the trip was in Penang, not more than four blocks from the Burmese Buddhist Temple. I was floored. This was not a coincidence as this was my spirit guide clearing the way for me to go. I asked my girlfriend if she wanted to endure the 24-hour flights back and forth, the unfamiliar food, the really hot weather, and constantly being around 30 people we didn't know. "There's nowhere else I would rather be." I booked it, and we waited nine months to take this guided tour.

The flight, hotels, food, and travel companions were all enjoyable and well done by the tour company. I was anxious the entire trip. I spoke to our guide and explained our reason for being on the trip. On the last day, we would have four hours on our own, and that's when Patti and I would go to the temple. Instead, our guide made the group's last stop at the Burmese temple. I was overwhelmed with gratitude, but he said he was honored to enable my quest.

Polished marble floors swooshed as we walked in our stockinged feet toward the 40-foot tall gold-highlighted Buddha. Birds chirped in the open air temple as I stood in silence, arms raised in anticipation,

Nothing in life has prepared me for this moment! There's no one I can ask. How do I call for those parts of me? How will I know them? How do I let them in?

Then I realized every experience, every moment, and every thought led me here. This was just one more path on my journey. In my mind's eye, I saw three golden orbs circle my head. Slowly, almost shyly, they entered my heart space. I was transfixed. Numb. Waking as if from a dream, my girlfriend by my side, we slowly walked back to the bus, the last to enter. Weeks after we returned, I still felt the changes within me.

I was open to what the Universe had in store for me. I was ready to accept where it would lead me. What could I do to make myself better? How could I help others? How could I be a better, more compassionate man?

I took Reiki courses to become a Reiki Master. I went to night school three nights a week to learn Polarity Therapy. I did weekend-long Theta Healing courses. Clients needing energetic clearing and healing came to me. I completed coaching courses. In writing courses, I recovered my teenage love of expression. I did daily yoga, writing, meditation, and clearing. My habits became rituals, manifesting presence.

Did I need to travel thousands of miles to find myself? I'll never know. But I learned through traveling that life is not the destination but the journey. Happiness is not where we are headed, it is a byproduct of living a full, compassionate, and heart-centered life: Shaking off all the shoulds, facing your failures, accepting your imperfection, and allowing all the wonder that is the world to be seen.

Seeing life through my mind's eye, I thought I was the master of time, outcome, reason, and judgment. Seeing life now through my heart, I know I am master only of me. Accepting, present, and at peace. Finally.

R. Scott Holmes, Energy Healing Practitioner and Transformational Coach. No matter the emotional, energetic, spiritual or physical roadblocks you encounter, there is a path to healing and clarity leading to understanding and joy.

The Healing Journey uses Reiki, Polarity Therapy, RYSE, and Theta Healing techniques to clear your sublime energetic system. Tools such as yoga, crystals, meditations, sound, journaling, and therapeutic oils are used to help you establish daily rituals. Finding the right tools and working with intention allows your body and spirit to heal and transform in miraculous ways.

If you want to live beyond the limits of human experience.

Seek and experience self-alignment to live fully.

Shift your values and focus to serving others.

Move through the fear that has limited your life, goals, and joy.

Find your voice for full expression.

Contact me and find that starting point

Website: Rscottholmes.com

Email: rscott_holmes@yahoo.com

Facebook: Find Your Voice, Transcendent Men

https://www.facebook.com/groups/355370599667931/

Instagram: r.scottholmes

Hosting Men's Group sessions via Zoom twice a month.
Private client sessions by request.

CHAPTER 2

RECOVERING THOU

THE GRACE IN AGING, THE SACRED SELF

Guy Kilchrist

Little boy feels loved, not as much.
Teen gets attention, not as much.
Young man in the world, a little too much.
Elder man naïve, not as much.
Today, I am. . .

I was following my dad to the barnyard; "Daddy, Daddy! When can I start milking the cow?" He says, "Son, when you are ten years old."

"But Daddy, I'm almost ten."

"Listen, son; I said when you're ten."

On my birthday, I could not wait for Dad to come home from work. I grabbed the milk bucket and headed to the barn. Our milk cow was waiting at the barn door. I opened it, and she went straight to the feed trough. After milking three teats, I reunite the suckling calf with its momma. After bringing the fresh milk into the house, I returned to separate the calf, who did not want to be separated from its momma. It was a wrestling match that got the best of me.

It took three days to realize it was not the fun I had imagined. I told Dad I didn't want to milk the cow anymore. He said, "Son, you're now ten years old; it's your chore, go milk the cow." I took one step out of childhood, didn't like it, and was not allowed to step back.

The next step came a year later: Catholic Confirmation. It was the same faith ritual generations of my family passed through and a means of belonging. After being coached by teachers and adult religious, I sat with my classmates in the front pews of St. Leo the Great Catholic Church to publicly voice my decision to follow Christ, even to a martyr's death.

It was presented as a choice, but there was never a thought of saying "no." When the moment arrived, I gave my commitment and immediately felt a frisson across my entire body, and in my mind's eye could visualize tongues of fire from above. Like my biblical hero, the wise King Solomon, I asked God for holy wisdom over all the gold in the world.

I've since asked many people about their Confirmation, and most say it was a non-spiritual event, hardly remembered. So, was my experience simply imagination and naivete—who can say? As a child, I opened my heart for God's spirit to dwell. Ever since, Indwelling Presence has been my companion and counselor through the highest joys and lowest moments of life.

The closeness of Cajun family culture permeated my childhood: loving grandparents, aunts, uncles, and cousins. Parental values centered around work, learning a trade, keeping one's word, helping others in need, and practicing the Catholic faith. Dad once shared that he trusted people upfront, and if they happened to betray that trust, he felt able to withstand the blow. As a young boy, I took hold of this and thus never became good, nor had the energy, at second-guessing people. My youth was primarily spent in the background observing the abilities and attention given to siblings and schoolmates. I often thought myself less capable than others and, with a bit of envy, wanted the ability to do things that others could do.

After high school, I followed the path of my dad and uncles. I joined the military and circled the globe by sea and air. Cajun boy had entered the big open, and promiscuous world of sex, drugs, and rock'n roll. With pride, I considered it a better version of a college education. I experienced the diversity of people, culture, and the good and not so good of this world. And out of ignorance, I often followed fools much braver than me. At the time, it all seemed harmless. It was not.

On my day of discharge, several close friends gave me a ride to the Honolulu airport. In the parking lot, we smoked our last joint together.

They handed me a stash to take home but apologetically refused, saying, "It was something I need to leave behind."

I entered university and, in my final year, met a woman with a four-year-old son. Four months later, I became a husband and dad. It seemed timely and logical, and I was tired of being single. Soon after that, we added a son and daughter. I envisioned my marriage and family life according to the ideals of my childhood: father and mother living together, raising children, then grandparenting, and ultimately death. I even imagined our end-of-life gravesite: husband and wife buried together.

Into my thirties came a nagging sense of something missing, and I felt my alcohol and tobacco consumption were obstacles to figuring it out. I liked the buzz but not the psychological dependency. After waking one morning with a splitting Vodka headache, I thought: *That's it! I don't want this anymore.* I quit tobacco cold turkey and, for the next 12 years, alcohol. I also returned to Sunday Mass but went alone to avoid a significant marital conflict.

Abstinence from alcohol opened space and time to know and accept me more deeply. I learned something good about myself but it did nothing to heal a deteriorating marriage. Four years later, I moved out and was forced into the court system to protect my role and time with my children.

Six months into the separation, I woke from a dream where I am standing on the edge of a grand cliff overlooking the open grandeur of deep space and time. My arms outstretched, and before me, in visual splendor, are the galaxies and emptiness of dark matter. I become dream conscious of eternity and the finality of death—my death. I awaken in deep anxiety.

It was 2 a.m., and I paced the floor, wondering if I was losing my mind. I even walked outside in the twilight, hoping to calm myself. The darkness of the night was suffocating. I needed daylight and someone with whom to talk. I thought of calling my mother but decided against it. It would have put her and Dad in a difficult position; I had to find a way to *stick it out* alone.

I return to bed, hoping to sleep but begin shivering uncontrollably. All I could think to do was pray. I recite the Lord's Prayer repeatedly, and the next thing I know, the alarm goes off, and it's morning. I feel fine. It was not a nightmare, but scary enough. It was a simple dream of sheer grace that brought into consciousness a much deeper and foundational context for the remainder of my life.

Six months later, my family fantasy of marriage, "till death do us part," was forever shattered in divorce court. I failed to give my children an upbringing in whole family unity, and ultimately had to forgive myself. I prayed, *God, my children need their father, and I need them. Keep me alive till they're grown and on their own.* The following weekend, I attended a retreat of talks, reflection, and group sharing with others who were also grieving the loss of a spouse through divorce, separation, or death.

In that one weekend, a small group of strangers opened and shared their hearts, souls, tears, and vulnerabilities. It was my first experience of authentic intimacy. On the last day, each person wrote their name atop a blank sheet and passed it to the person on their right. We each took a moment to write a heartfelt reflection about the person whose name was affixed.

Four strangers saw in me a good and caring man—who loves and deserves love. I cried, wondering how I lost or never held that same sense of self-worth. It was a new beginning experience. Now single, I chose celibacy to give my children the focus of love, time, and energy they needed from their father and not fall into the same trap of sexual relationships. I did not close myself off from female friendships, but sexual intimacies would only be a byproduct of long-term companionship and marriage. I devoted much of my alone time to fulfilling a childhood desire to play guitar. I joined a church folk choir to learn guitar while overcoming the insecurity of expressing my spirituality and prayer in public. And it did.

Ten years later, my children reach maturity, and I'm introduced to a wonderful woman. After a three-year courtship, we join in marital union.

Earlier in the year, my father died unexpectedly. I found him face-down behind the barn. When I turned him over, I saw by his face that he was gone. It was a visual image and moment for his son alone. I had my solitary and final conversation with him and, in our typical father-son banter, asked and fussed why he thought it was okay to leave now since we had just finished cleaning up around the old barn. I received my father's death, the selling of his cows, and the way it unfolded as his final lesson and gift of grace. Now into my fifties, I began seeing myself in a different light, independent of my father's beloved presence.

After our Church wedding, our reception begins by acknowledging our deceased parents and expressing gratitude to our collective friends and family for their presence. Soon after the music starts, my loving bride, totally out of character, takes center stage and sings her rendition of the 1960s hit, *My Guy:* "There's nothing you can do, could make me untrue to my guy, there's nothing you could buy, could make me tell a lie to my guy." I stood in front of the bandstand in complete awe and love. I had no reason to doubt her.

Days after returning from our honeymoon, I receive notice of a pending severance from my 22-year employment, three years short of retirement benefits. It was a betrayal of sorts, and once again, I had to rebuild a fresh vision for life, now in marital union.

In the following ten years, we begin each morning with a hug and kiss. And our days are absent of marital conflict. We were both retired, had lived a lifetime of Catholic tradition, and were heavily involved in church ministry. Five years into the marriage, we entered the deacon formation program as a willing couple. It was a huge decision and a five-year formation process.

At ordination, I lay prostrate in front of the cathedral altar, publicly professing my vow of obedience to God's Word. Afterward, I begin serving in the community of my home parish.

Later in that year, I recall walking alone in our backyard, feeling gifted with the best of married love, a desire to study and teach the gospel, and in a position to serve those who come to the church in their need. I thought how fortunate it had all come. Three months later, on a fateful Wednesday morning, it crashed.

After returning home from serving at Mass, I'm handed a typed letter from my spouse and told to read it. It says, "I am unhappy, fearful of you, and will soon move in with my son." As I read, I'm shoved into another world.

That evening, I asked, "This fear you write about, are you afraid I am going to physically hurt you in some way? She replied, "No, not at all." Then, what is it? She had no emotion, no tears, just silence. It was a voiceless answer, and it broke my heart. The best of who I am was not enough.

The following morning, after a sleepless night, I asked her not to leave. Two days later, she packed her car and returned to her son. All I could do was accept. Three days later, I'm ordered by the diocese to end and disconnect from all parish and public church ministry, effectively severing hundreds of relationships and obligations. I'm told to go home to a crushing emptiness.

Married life, church community life, and ministerial relationships vanished in three days. Having been so abruptly erased from public view, the gossip and suspicions of my character began to fly. I felt crumpled, put in a cage, and thrown into a dark corner. I was cut deeply by another and then cut again. My willingness to believe and trust in the core good of humanity and the institutional church disappeared.

Under this weight, I insisted I be kind to myself in all ways. I would not accept or participate in shame or self-worthlessness. I would keep open to the world, even though I was struggling with humanity that I no longer felt was good at its core. I stepped deeper into literary and visual art as a method of expression, healing, and keeping open to the larger world via my website. (www.graceinarts.com)

The divorce was finalized in a year, but my future status with the diocese remained in limbo. One morning, I realized the hard truth of my institutional insignificance and could no longer entrust the hierarchy with my well-being. It brought me to my lowest and most painful point. I cry out to God for one thing; that this deep well of loneliness and grief—not be wasted.

I take a month to discern, then tell the diocesan office that I cannot heal in a cage and request resolution of my clerical status and ministry. I'm later told, "It was not our intent to harm you. You've done nothing wrong." Two years later, I received an official letter expressing appreciation for doing everything asked of me—the verdict: retired with no liturgical, sacramental, or teaching authority. As if I am now worthless. My voice and sacramental identity are to be denied and hidden within church walls. Truth, justice, and charity had no currency.

Cast out into the metaphorical desert, I began deconstructing what I thought these relationships had been. My starting place was the statement found in my beloved's fateful letter, "I have not been honest." I misjudged what I thought was the truth. I had to first forgive myself for believing in that which was not, nor could ever be. It was my idolatry, of sorts. And in this dark night, encountering God alone, I discovered my poverty, my sacredness.

Not time nor treasure, not even talents to give, but being itself.
Nothing to do in this naked awareness but consent to love.
Harvest first fruit, along its path . . .poverty fulfilled.

In Acts of the Apostle (8:26), Phillip, one of the original seven deacons, hears an angel of the Lord, "Go south to the road – the desert road. . ." I also heard it. I began reading the lives and teachings of the desert mothers and fathers, St. Benedict, Teresa of Avila, John of the Cross, Meister Eckhart, Thomas Merton, and others. It led me to a better understanding of the first beatitude (Matt 5:3) and the contemplative path of kenosis—a self-emptying of that which is no longer life-giving.

In this dark night, seat of my soul
Keep holy the clay of my feet and hands
Rest my senses, my thoughts – in the heart
Silent consent of Divine Presence and Action
Sings the bowl, to the hearings of this world
Breathe anew, smile again.

I am no longer as naïve about trusting in the good of others, but each day, I remind myself that I, and we, have the innate capacity to manifest God because we already are that image by virtue of being created.

Having been conceived through the Creator's love is my birthright. It's not to be ignored, given away, or taken away. So, when the inner critic or other person tries to convince me otherwise—I am to insist on safeguarding my person, conscience, and soul. It's a graceful act of sacred self-love and the calling of Holy Wisdom.

In my former Navy days, we often shouted, "Make a hole!" It meant to create a space or passageway for someone or some critical activity. Today, the meaning takes on a new twist: "Make a whole." It is to clear space in my life for what is needed for wholeness: slowing down and consuming less, embracing solitude and listening deeply, hallowing my diminishments, and nurturing soul-consciousness. All in accordance with the communion of souls, both past and present.

I keep and honor the sacred identity of a beloved son, brother, father, and friend but retire from roles demanding I stand front and center to analyze and solve problems, teach, preach, or lead. I worked hard and long to be good at those things, but their purpose has been fulfilled. And I no longer need or want those meanings in my life. It is a time for fruitful unbinding.

It's hard for sure, maybe impossible, to fully forgive another person, or institution, especially when one never hears "I am sorry" or any attempts at reconciliation. It's as if the harm done remains active. Over time, these flesh-burning wounds stack, making it difficult to keep one's heart open and loving.

In scripture, Jesus says, forgive seventy times seven. He also said: "Father, forgive them, for they do not know what they are doing." (Luke 23:34). In his most painful and dying moments, he did not say, "I forgive them." He directly asked the Creator of heaven and earth to forgive them. Maybe the moment was too much for his humanity.

Today, I am enough, and now know I have always been. Loving my sacred self in each moment as it is, requires accepting and forgiving the limitations of my humanity. And by surrendering to God, the remnants of my unforgiveness (both to self and others) sets my spirit free.

May others have the heart and will to do the same.

We are all endowed with a creative spirit. How you and I express ourselves in each moment is our original art and cannot be reproduced by anyone else. Sometimes it is inspiring and beyond words; sometimes, not so much. Either way, it's worthy of being shown, not hidden.

I grew up in a household where creativity was not just for artistic pursuits but also a critical life skill. Both Mom and Dad were gifted in what they could do with their hands. And they passed it on to their children.

My life, much like my art, is an exploration. Sometimes serious, sometimes playful. My creative spirit and curiosity have been the underlying motive in my engineering, education, and ministry work. Nowadays, my visual and literary art is just another language I speak. When my creative spirit is active, and at play, I feel alive and amazed.

I began my artistic endeavors as a 12-year-old when I redeemed 30 dum-dum wrappers for a rudimentary camera and took my first roll of film. Since, I've had roles in aerial photography, event and studio work, and university photographer. In later years, I began studying egg tempera and sacred iconography. Nowadays, I've branched into an expressionistic visual and literary exploration incorporating many mediums (www.graceinarts.com).

In life and art, I desire to maintain loose boundaries of inquiry, exploration, imagination, creativity, and service. I strive to be open, honest, and heartfelt with myself and others and to cooperate in grace, the life-giving spirit of it all—to take me where it wills.

I am over-joyed in family, fatherhood, and sacred friendship. And most relaxed when the pace of my life is five mph slower than the speed limit.

CHAPTER 3

REDEFINING HAROLD

SEARCHING FOR TRUTH, IDENTITY, AND REDEMPTION

James Kealiipiilani Kawainui,
Native Hawaiian Healer, Mentor, Kahu[1]

My birth father remains a mystery to me. He and my mother met in the Army. Aside from contributing his DNA and eventually knowing his name, what I learned from my mom, or dug up on the internet, we had no connection. He made it perfectly clear he wanted no part of my mother or me and walked away before I was born.

Not knowing who he was has haunted me my entire life. I made the assumption early on that whatever happened between them might be too painful a memory for her, so it remained a question in my mind until I was 48 years old. It only came to the surface after I moved to New Zealand and met Lui.

For most of my life I've felt abandoned and unwanted. As I embarked on my healing journey, I opened the door to my connection with my Kūpuna[2] and started my healing practice. I became keenly aware of how the early events of my life had impacted who I'd become. This was the legacy I'd inherited from Harley and one my stepfather Harold fostered.

I went to live with Harold and my mom when I was four and a half years old. My grandmother, who adopted me as an infant, suffered a stroke and

1 Hawaiian for Priest
2 Ancestors in Hawaiian

could no longer care for herself or me. They already had three children, and Harold was quick to point out that I was an unwelcome burden. "Nobody wants you, so we're stuck with you. I'm stuck with you." My mom not only had an abusive husband to contend with but four children under five years old.

I felt insignificant and alone. There was Harold and his family, and there was me. I don't remember feeling loved, supported, or safe at home. There were no hugs or words of encouragement, only Harold's constant salvo of physical and psychological abuse.

From the moment I went to live with them, he drilled into me how stupid and useless I was. Nothing I did was ever good enough for Harold. He laid the foundation that became my truth. I continued to hear Harold's voice in my head long after I'd left home. He'd become part of my internal guidance system and the first to dole out criticism and judgment. I had little or no self-confidence and was my own worst critic, which showed in everything I did.

It wasn't until I went to New Zealand and started working with my mentor Lui that I was able to unwind from my childhood and safely look at the trauma.

*

"You're going to New Zealand," I heard my Kūpuna say one day out of the blue. *How is that possible? How am I supposed to get there?* My answer came a few weeks later when a friend, who was from New Zealand, asked me if I'd go with her. Who was I to say no?

As I got off the plane, I heard the voice of my ancestors once again. *Settle in,* they said. *You're going to be here for a while.* A three-month trip turned into five and a half years. I didn't have a clue why I was there but knew enough to realize they had a plan for me; it just hadn't been revealed yet.

I vividly remember the night I met Lui. Someone at a sweat lodge I went to told me about a Māori Healer teaching a class on Māori Spirituality. "You should come," she said. "I think you'll find it interesting." I showed up at the Titirangi Community Center and saw a man sitting at the front of the room. He looked me straight in the eye as I walked in. "Good," he said. "We've been waiting for you." *Who's been waiting for me? What the hell is he talking about?* I didn't know this man from Adam, but he acted as though he knew me.

From the moment we met, Lui took me under his wing and opened me up to a world that I sensed was there but hadn't known how to access. Under his tutelage, I learned the healing ways of the Māori lineage he carried. It was only as we began to uncover the trauma of my past that I finally began to face the things I'd spent my whole life avoiding.

I'll never forget my first healing session with Lui. The Māori have an intense style of bodywork called Romiromi; it's like Rolfing[3] on steroids. It was the most excruciating experience of my life. For over two hours it felt like he, and the two brutes he enlisted to help him, were ripping me apart. The pain was blinding. "Your resistance is what's making this so painful, Bro. I'm not stopping until you let go." I kept fighting him until fatigue overtook me, and I finally gave in. A burst of energy surged through my body that I didn't know was possible. I felt every cell vibrating and saw myself as pure light. Laying there in an altered state, I met two guardians who've become part of my Etheric Team. In opposite corners, watching over me, were a fully armored Samurai and an eight-foot-tall Hawaiian warrior.

I experienced longer periods of calm and peace after Lui's session than I'd never known before. The anger was still there, but it'd lost its grip. I saw how it controlled my life and was the driver behind the reactions and decisions I'd made over the years.

Through Lui's guidance and compassion, I understood how Harold's voice became my internal compass, pointing me to choices that continually undermined my self-confidence and self-worth. It was like watching me being me but from a different perspective. The language he taught me fueled my negative reactions until they became automatic. In order to resolve the inner conflict I was carrying, I had to let go of Harold.

As my perspective changed, I surprisingly found myself having compassion for Harold. His mother was a cruel human being, and I have no memories of her ever being happy. She ruled her family through

3 The Rolfing method is a structural integration form of bodywork that reorganizes the connective tissues, called fascia, that permeate the entire body. The process enables the body to regain the natural integrity of its form, thus enhancing postural efficiency and freedom of movement. It can be a very painful process and requires a series of ten sessions

intimidation and fear. Harold's siblings, all grown adults, were terrified of her. I hated being at her house and witnessing the verbal and emotional abuse directed at anyone on her bad side. No wonder Harold turned out the way he did. Look at the teacher he had. It didn't absolve what he'd done, but it did help me begin to unwind the anger. Lui taught me to recognize and catch myself and not sink back into familiar patterns. I watched my life slowly change.

The real surprise was my anger towards my mom. I was so busy focusing on Harold that I never saw it. I was angry that she never talked to me about my birth father. I was angry that she stayed married to Harold even after he'd beaten her when I was 12. I was angry she never protected us from him. She rarely intervened and would stand by, watch, and sometimes even encourage the punishing abuse he doled out to me and my siblings.

During a sweat lodge in New Zealand, we were all asked what we wanted most from the ceremony. I made a declaration shortly before we stepped into the inipi, "I'm ready to let go of all the anger and rage I've been holding on to and ask for your prayers during the ceremony." The sweat lodge lasted over three hours, and when we were done, I had cried, chanted, and sang everything I was holding on to and gave it all to the heat, the darkness, and the stones. Another layer of peace came over me during the last round that slowly settled over the next few weeks. Harold's voice became softer still, and I found myself not dropping into self-judgment as quickly as I had in the past.

Other aspects of my life began to change. My connection to my Kūpuna grew stronger. My days had more clarity, and when triggered, I found it easier to steer myself back into centered peace.

*

Lui taught me how our unconscious patterns run our lives. I saw the patterns in the people coming to me for healing work. Our childhood sets a precedent for how our lives will be. Our habits become lifelong patterns running unconsciously in the background because that's what our body, mind, and emotions have been entrained to do. The patterns become repetitive. As they are reinforced, our personalities are created. Most of what we learn, particularly if it's the result of trauma or traumatic events, helps mold a survival strategy that we'll refer to over and over again. That strategy embeds itself until it runs automatically, without our conscious awareness.

SELF-AWARENESS IS THE KEY TO CHANGE

If you're wondering how to break those patterns, the simple answer is that the more you become aware of how certain situations or emotions have repeated themselves in your life, the more likely you'll be able to shift them when they show up. Breaking down old habits so you can build new ones is a necessary part of the process. The more you're able to see how the pattern asserts itself, the better equipped you'll be to respond to them. It'll help you create new ways of thinking.

WORDS ARE SPELLS, BE CAREFUL HOW YOU USE THEM

Have you ever listened to the language you use to describe yourself and the world around you? Your words are powerful and have long-lasting effects, especially if you continue to use them to reinforce negativity. You're not unlucky, stupid, ugly, or unlovable. When you find yourself using negative words, I invite you to change them and find less damaging and more positive ways to express yourself. By changing your words, you change the energy and hopefully how you feel about yourself or the situation you're in. It takes practice and diligence, but this one small step will help establish positive new patterns.

CHANGE YOUR OUTLOOK, CHANGE YOUR OUTCOME

We often don't realize how our need for perfection, created partly because of our need to prove our self-worth, may trigger negative self-talk. You didn't make a mistake; you did something that didn't turn out as you'd expected or hoped. "Let me step back and see if I can find another way to get this done" is an affirmation I've adopted over the years. Instead of being critical, give yourself space to think about the obstacle or situation you're in. Finding a different approach may lead you to a better solution, taking the pressure off of having to be perfect.

ASKING FOR HELP IS A STRENGTH, NOT A WEAKNESS

Sometimes a habit or pattern runs so deep we need guidance and another pair of eyes to help us recognize and define it so we can overcome our old mindset. It's hard to see, let alone change something when you're in the middle of it. That's what Lui did for me. He was a neutral presence outside of myself. He saw things I couldn't see on my own. He gently and compassionately walked me through those dark places, always reminding me I wasn't alone or broken. He helped me see the patterns and taught me how to interrupt them and find other ways to move through them. I couldn't have done it without his help. Lui was the accountability partner I desperately needed to keep me on track and someone I could trust and rely on. His reassurance kept me going. Having his help was the smartest thing I've ever done for myself.

Seeking help is an act of self-love. Here's a link if you'd like to reach out and talk about a situation you've been stuck in that you're ready to change in your life. https://www.ancientwisdom4u.com/ancientwisdom4u/

*

Shortly after the sweat lodge, my mom asked me to come home to attend a family reunion with relatives we'd been out of touch with for three generations. Going home would be a chance to see how much I had changed because of the work I'd done with Lui. I felt like I was ready to see her and Harold.

The family reunion helped me fully align with my lineage and Hawaiian roots. We were all given a compilation of the genealogical research one of my cousins had done. In it were 16 generations of my family and ancestors. The depth of her research was remarkable, and I was grateful to finally have answers to who I was and where I came from.

I recognized the name of my grandfather, 16 generations removed from a book on Hawaiian history I'd read years before called *Ruling Chiefs of Hawaii*[4]. I went back to that book, found his name, and went back four more generations when I suddenly heard my Kūpuna say, *How much more proof do you need before you accept that this is who you are?* I closed the book and never looked back. It affirmed the path I'd taken and the decision to become a healing practitioner.

4 *Ruling Chiefs of Hawaii*, Samuel Kamakau, ©1961 & 1992 Kamehameha Schools/Bishop Estate

"I need to talk to you about something," I said to my mom shortly after I returned. "Tell me about my real dad. Who was he? Why did he leave? Where was he from?" She told me his name was Harley and talked about their relationship and his decision to walk away. I expressed my anger towards her for not telling me about him and not protecting me from Harold. "I felt so alone and unsupported growing up," I said. "I was just trying to keep everything together and take care of all of you and Grandma. I was just too tired most of the time," she replied. (Did I mention that I'm the oldest of eight children?) "I'm sorry," she said. "I never meant for any of that to happen to you."

I didn't realize my grandmother had come to live with her at the same time I did. The adult version of me understood, but it was the little kid who had been holding on all those years. I felt that part of me soften and heard him say, "I love you. I forgive you." She smiled through the tears as we hugged each other.

We spoke more frequently after that, and I said I love you more often. They weren't empty words anymore; they came from my heart.

Harold was a little more elusive. He still felt unapproachable. His health was declining, and he spent all his days and nights in his La-Z-Boy in front of his TV. By then, he was just a shadow of the person I used to know. All that was left was a feeble and bitter old man who'd withdrawn into his own inner world. Our conversations were superficial at best. I tried several times but never found the doorway. My anger didn't have an edge to it anymore. I'd done the letting go in New Zealand, and there wasn't a pull to react, which I found strangely calming. I realized I'd taken my power back.

It was my last day there, and I was headed to the airport. "I'm leaving, Dad. I just wanted to come and say goodbye." When will I see you again?" he asked. "In a few months," I said. "I love you, Dad, and I forgive you," I blurted out. It wasn't anything I'd planned. It felt natural. Tears streaming down his cheeks, he reached out and grabbed my hand. He didn't say anything and just held on for a few seconds. "I love you too," he said through the tears. I bent over and kissed him on the cheek. Everything we had experienced together in our lives resolved itself at that moment. I felt the old bonds break and a sense of peace come over us. I knew my letting go had created the space for this moment, and without it, none of this would've happened.

I only saw Harold twice more before he left his body. Each time he would cry and hold my hand. I would always reassure him that I loved him. Because I moved to the Mainland, and my mom had put him in managed care, we didn't get to talk much. There wasn't anything else to say. I was grateful that we'd both come to a peaceful place.

Years later, as I reflected on my life, I realized the gifts Harold gave me as a kid. Even though they originally were survival skills, I use them every day and rely on them to help my clients. My empathic abilities developed because of him. I had to know how he was feeling quickly, and it got to the point that I knew his mood even before he drove up our driveway. My childhood experiences helped nurture a deep sense of compassion. I know what it feels like to be in dark situations and go through tough times. I can talk to people in a way that lets them know that I understand their pain, creating a bridge that helps build trust. Who would've thought something which began as a negative would turn into such a positive in my life?

Are the demons completely gone? No. But I've found another way to live my life, no longer trapped inside a mind that was hell-bent on tearing me down. I'm grateful I get to share the wisdom and knowledge of my Kūpuna everyday with the people coming to me for help. I have great love and gratitude to Lui for giving me another way of looking at my life and my Kūpuna for their continued guidance and direction. I especially feel blessed that I can serve others with all that I've learned.

Me Ke Aloha Pumehana[5],

James.

---

5 Translation: With all the love in my heart

James Kawainui is a Native Hawaiian Healer, Mentor, and Kahu with family roots going back over 20 generations in Hawaii. His family is the shaman of his culture, and he shares that ancient wisdom with the people that come to him for help.

James' awakening came over 20 years ago when he first heard his Kūpuna (ancestors). *It's time to go home,* they said. He listened and walked away from a successful corporate career and moved back to Hawaii. Since then, his journey has been to understand his gifts on innumerable levels.

James is a spiritual strategist and works comprehensively with people who are on a personal journey to understand the deeper and oftentimes hidden parts of themselves by sharing practices, techniques, and insights that help people live their lives with more clarity, conviction, and purpose.

James is also an expert in the causes and long-term effects of trauma, PTSD, chronic pain, stress, anxiety, and depression and works with people on resetting the generational programming and self-limiting belief systems that have defined their lives.

James' clients come from many walks of life and all parts of the globe. Their personal or professional backgrounds are often driven by a need to find inner peace, clarity, and focus in their lives and a desire to understand their existence.

If you're ready to explore how James can help you overcome the obstacles which keep holding you back so you can find deeper meaning in your life, and connect with your passion and purpose, schedule your free 30 minutes Find Your Ancient Wisdom Discovery call, use this link:

Find your Ancient Wisdom

https://www.ancientwisdom4u.com/self-love-meditation/

CHAPTER 4

HEALING THE FATHER ARCHETYPE

RECLAIMING VITALITY AND SUCCESS

Dan Gorbunow, AMT

It was March in the north country, and the air was cold and dry with heavy snow and ice patches on the ground. Puffs of vapor spewed from buildings in the federal prison camp in the sub-zero temperatures as bundled men sought refuge, food, and warmth in a maze of daily activity. I was in a state of numb submission. Many guys who arrived there, like me, walked themselves through the security door to the camp or had long before yielded to institutionalization and were weaning themselves slowly out. I walked in with eyes wide open, mouth shut.

I will emerge from this a stronger person. I accept no label, no judgment, no curse. My actions have created this situation, and my actions will change it.

It was not a harsh environment like what is typically shown in the movies, not a max or super-max with armed guards and patrols on towers. It was prison-light, a calm compound of salty characters, often resilient and respectful. Men coexisted peacefully on the edge of a knife, paying penance for a felony, typically drug possession, theft, fraud, and usually non-violent offenses. I did not feel unsafe for the most part, yet at the outset, I was morbid, muted, and withdrawn, my chest and limbs heavy. Aside from generalized inner turmoil bound up in the faces of other inmates, the most dangerous thing visible on the compound were provisions delivered by truck to the kitchen in boxes marked *"Not fit for consumption."*

Oh yum.

On the third day after arrival, I ventured to the community building to locate the library—a symbol of liberation, of escape from detention into knowledge. The library was a disheveled walk-in closet stuffed to the gills with gobs of tired fiction, batches of cracked self-help books, a rack of heavy legal books, worn 12-steps and bibles, parenting, and finance.

"Nope. Nope. Not now. No thanks. Not any of these, none of those. Maybe later." (In Scottish dialect) "Is there anythin' worth salvaging in all this *crrrap?*"

I was determined to fish out at least one good book to dive into. I kept to task, uncovering a few boxes of hidden books under piles of King, Steele, and Clancy then found the juicy nugget I was looking for. It almost leaped into my hands, *Iron John: A Book About Men,* by Robert Bly.

"Hmm. Come here, my darling, let me take a look at you."

I opened it for the first time and paged through hastily.

What manner of brain-spawn are you? I was intrigued.

This will do.

I was content with my find, so I bundled myself up for the cold walk across the camp to my dorm and bunk, carrying the book in my coat like a wolf coveting a forgotten bone in its jaws. I quietly chewed on it for months.

I maintained myself detached and complicit, propping myself up to cope with the daily grind. Bly, his book, was my closest friend, consoling with a dependable cup of sage tea and rousing with realizations like thunderbolts.

I learned there was a forgotten Earth Father within the cosmos, nature, and culture. In complement to the lofty, well-known sky father, a hidden Zeus of nature and magic lay dormant in men. The exiled Divine Masculine presence prowls in the bogs of old forests and mossy ruins of myth and psyche, patiently waiting to be scooped out. Grief accompanies him in the wilderness beyond the pale, past what is comfortably familiar. Meeting him is to go on a journey, to wander into the woods.

I have been here before, in my soul, dreams, and memories.

Iron John uncovers our collective losses and shows where we are hurt. The sore shoulders of modern people bear the weight of sadness and exile from the deep self, from the hidden father.

Suffering a deficiency syndrome of some essential bio-psycho-social substance, a vital father nutrient is missing in us. His absence is exacerbated by disconnection to the Sacred Feminine. The male and female principles descend together, so we are dually afflicted. The costs to all of us for the compounded impairments of the soul are staggering.

Thunderclaps in my chest. I was not alone in my ache and deficit of father, in each of his three dimensions—biological, cultural, and archetypal—all distant, displaced. Cawing in the marsh like a crow, Bly calls out a vast cultural diaspora of soul-hungry men. Visible proof of semi-conscious, dad-deficient men lie around and within me. Men stranded like me, caught in the belly of a great invisible whale. It disguised itself as addiction, dysfunction, incarceration, broken families, and broken hearts. Beyond grief, other strangers await us in the dark.

Fortunately, though still out of sight, there is a golden well of abundance abiding in our very nature. The forgotten elder in the pond arrives *with many gifts and treasures,* it is told, *more gold and silver than you can imagine.* A hidden talent gleams in the tangled hair and muck. I can feel it in me and observe it in others.

I have a map—a way out of this conundrum, a tome of beauty and legend and insight. How many of you men would go with me? For now, I am going alone. I have to help myself first.

Time marched on in a forgotten place as the old life quietly dissolved. Disintegration was palpable in the herd of shuffles, like clockwork, to the mess hall, in the dull food I ate, in the drab silence of study, in the workout room where men used iron to subdue pain and tension, in the anxious crowd of men at mail call, in the long hours of nights in concrete and grief. Wisdom pulls you into its jaws and digests you slowly.

Without warning, a flower of new understanding emerged, sweet like the first smell of soil in April thaw, distinct like a clarion of remembrance. My spirit began to return, taking notes and offering insights and poems.

Are we men voracious consumers or the voraciously consumed? Maybe we are Ourobouros—the snake devouring and rebirthing itself endlessly.

Something in us is driving the program of our life. If we can make it conscious, we have a chance of restoring ourselves and avoiding the pitfalls. Until then, it can operate as a black hole that distorts or steals light and energy. The distortions I operated with for all my adult life had finally engulfed me. I was drowning in slow-motion, stuck in the marshes of unexamined subconscious material. Somewhere in us, a king hungers for spirit, self, and connection.

Seasons passed, I turned a corner, and radical honesty grabbed my throat. I decided to look courageously into my entire life story and the difficult territory I landed in and to glean a way through it. A void that ate half my childhood threatened my hopes for fatherhood, and I was perched at its doorstep. I sought company and connection to help me forward, but not always successfully.

I wrote to my father and did not get any reply. I wrote letters to my estranged young son's mother, who I found out moved out of state without telling me, taking him (two years old) to Hawaii. She did not respond either. It was excruciating. Alas, everyone was a thousand miles away in a world I could not reach.

I am a bird struck in the road breathing his dying breath, waiting for something to pick me up. No father, no son, no breath, no tears left—only candle-less vigils in the abyss and pale moons beyond prison glass.

My studies offered a way through, salted my appetite for understanding and *gnosis,* and whet my thirst for resolution. I knew all these things were tied together. I wrote and prayed a lot.

I was being purged into a cold hell, not of blazing fire but of dark water, the deep interior of the psyche. Suspended in the depths, I was grateful to have a poet-wizard nearby. Bly handed me a sturdy old bucket; *Extraction* stamped in crimson rust. It was roomy enough for my questions, hopes, sorrows, fantasies, and even truth. I commenced bucketing, the process of going in and pulling out energy and information from shadow—subconscious, lost parts of self.

The inner sludge is difficult to peruse and accept. Arrogance, ego, and defensiveness in my personality demanded urgent remediation. Beneath them was a thin-skinned adolescence, a hallow uncertainty that disputed any confidence and belief in self. The underlying message at the bottom, conjected by my father's neglect, said *I don't matter.* Vulnerability added layers of protection.

Golden boy, my *puer,* the escape artist and instigator, was dragged forward for cross-examination. The immature puer aeternus, prone to pleasure-seeking, seeks flight from the demands of discipline and the rigors of responsibilities. Unable to recognize his inner gold, his low esteem is bolstered by grandiosity. Worse, his efforts and energy are often plundered by his own impulsivity. In the watery ripples, I witness myself struggling, restless, face distraught, eyes lit, hunting relentlessly for validation or dissolution.

How long have I chased the nameless void, seeking fulfillment?

More scoops—candlelit meetings at the pond with my emotionally distant dad. Peering into the water, I see my dad's shame and addiction, his father's grief, and alcoholism. In the mossy underworld, there's me alongside them.

I'm just like you guys. Is my little boy next?

Spiral threads interlace a Celtic knot-work of fathers and ancestors with a third spool, my ailing outer quest to reconnect with my infant son, who was carried off to distant islands. I feel a hole in my ribs where a father's grief resides; salty tears burn my eyes holding back pressure and frustration.

I'm on my way for you, son. Know that I am here.

Pulling up from the deep, I eventually fished out a rusty iron chain forged of shadow, absence, and hurt that was who-knows-how-many generations-long running through my lineage. My ache signaled to me that I had hit bottom.

Somewhere, in a place of no place, some time, in a time of no-time, some man, in a group of no-men, I lay awake. In the lonesome nights of my soul's inquiries, a clear desire arose in me to break the rusted chain, claim the forgotten ore within, and forge myself anew.

I am going to pull myself out of this fucking mire!

Ready to change my life, I knew in order to be balanced, healthy, and successful, I must retrieve my lost father experience. Not just that vacant guy, my biological dad, but also the energy and archetype of the father. The cup of the king was dry, and hydration could not be delayed any further.

A rhythm of physical and mental activity in camp emerged as I processed my life stories. I was cleansing, learning, reclaiming. Cleansing a memory of childhood injury and a failed father image caught in the deep, I was learning the way to navigate and decipher the story of my early life. Reclaiming the mythic vitality of masculine energy in my psyche, I found hope for a way through my conditions.

It all came together one day, and my world got a lot brighter when the new man showed up, the one who would help me govern the man I was becoming, offering me a golden opportunity to heal what was long hidden. I was lying in my bunk, daydreaming, in the late afternoon with the dorm room to myself.

I recalled a period in my early childhood, spending time with my father in his Uptown apartment, along with TV sports, sci-fi books, and a hi-fi stereo. I don't remember much dad warmth there. He was an emotional Houdini, disappearing in plain sight of me. I recalled a moment and saw myself, age seven, standing behind him as he sat on the couch. He was puffing on a bong, watching the game on TV. Silent, standing there, baseball in my hands, I wanted to ask him to play with me, but I felt that his head was not in the game of fathering. I lost the desire to ask and fell into a trance.

Could I cut the dead head off of Dad and transplant it with a living one that took more interest in me?

Imaginative young minds want to know. The hurt memory invited me to do something about it, about the void I was carrying. I saw with new eyes and clarity. There was no loving, inspiring Zeus-father in the memory, no useful blueprint for healthy masculinity, only a nameless shame lodged in stone.

I must excavate and restore the lost father out of the quarry of self.

Guided by necessity and instinct, I edited the memory. I was ready to heal.

I embarked at the precise moment of disassociation. That's important. Poison is extracted out through the same wound as it entered. In my imagination, I returned to the scene, turned about, then followed the hallway to the back of Dad's apartment, toward the den where I would sometimes play and console myself. In place of the den, I suddenly beheld a doorway opening to a beautiful hidden courtyard. Excited and curious, my mind produced this new material without effort. The dormitory seemed miles away.

Into the imaginary courtyard, I walked in wonder. It was magnificent, full of wild birds, fluorescent peacocks, and sunlight. Pine scented mountain air percolated with clear spring water through marble fountains. The azure sky and billowy clouds hosted sunbeams and thunderstorms. I felt a deep peace and life force resonating in the architecture, beauty, and wildness all around. I beheld the silhouette of a tall man standing in the archway before me. His features materialized as I approached: bearded like waves of salt and fields of braided wheat, his eyes shone with warmth, respect, and appreciation. He welcomed me toward him with the outstretched hands and arms of a loving king, and I embraced him. At that moment, I connected with my healthy inner father, a holy archetype, received his blessings, and was instantly filled with energy. I felt a deep homecoming within me and noticed joy, a tingling everywhere in my body, heart, and spirit. Something the hurt, hungry boy wanted all my life was granted. The stone cracked, letting light in.

I carried the energy of this exchange with me. I thanked Divine king-father in the courtyard as I retraced my way to the vacant hallway of Dad's apartment. Imagination rolled on.

Shadow-dad was still there, watching the game, hitting his pipe, as if nothing had changed, except I had changed. I was radically different, electric and tall. Poised between these two fathers, shadow and light, I silently declared my bond to the caring, present king-father.

This is my father!

I opened my eyes, sat up, still alone in my dorm, and gave it some voice.

"This is my father!" I proclaimed out loud and stood up. I addressed the other guy in my vision, the addict, the man in the box, and cut the air with,

"Fuck you, Dad!"

I shook; the words rang like steel on stone. My face was hot.

"Sorry, man, you gotta go!" I whispered. Pent energy coursed through my whole body, sending shards of emotional debris flying, bits of rage and hurt hitting the walls of the prison, burning holes. Rays of light poked through.

"You don't seem to give a fuck about me. This boy needs more. He *is* *more* than this!" I hissed into the void, dispelling the vision. I had just felled a giant, and the bigness of that bore through me. I was spiritually awake and physically exhausted.

I quieted down, let the holy fire simmer, lay back, and faded out. I roused later as my bunkmate woke me up for the dinner call. I recalled my vision, felt my breath expanding with a deep, peaceful presence, and gave notice to Shadow-dad:

Looking over the years of self, struggling, I feel you in there, old man, in the absence and empty spaces. I hereby release you! I claim full responsibility for fathering. It's on me now. For whatever gifts you gave me, thank you. Goodbye.

"See you, not gonna be you. Anymore."

How have I lived so long in the dark, half a life?

The wild man of iron in the deep helped me to access a hidden golden father and purify my shadow. The rusty chain broke, and the skin of a snake peeled off, pouring light into the vacancy; a new power awakened. The voice of a reclaimed Divine king father emerged, alive with spirit and joyful resonance.

There is nothing we cannot achieve, so dream big! Go forth, brilliant light, and make this world a place of beauty, healing, and wonder. You rock!

I began to appreciate the man in the mirror. More smiles, fewer frowns. He's a good guy. I'm excited for him and what he accomplishes. The eyes once lit with a hungry void now enjoy vitality and warmth, inner confidence radiating out into the world. The Divine beauty is more visible to me in the unfolding experiences of life, like sparks in the heart of every man I meet, in each blade of new grass, in the call of wild gander in the spring.

There is a season for everything, and each man has his own path to take, to answer the void however he will. Forgiving, honoring, accepting. The hidden force within me released a flow of creative powers to attract all that I desired, more than imaginable. Successes grew in all parts of my life, work, family, and mission.

In the weave of my new life, time offered to settle old accounts. One day the lost boy returned, a chance for father and son to reconcile. Nearly a man, my son beheld his father standing in the doorway, with a beard of salt and an unfettered smile of joy. My arms outstretched like a loving king, heart full of sunbeams and thunderbolts, I looked into my son's eyes and embraced him. The last chard of rust fell.

"Welcome home!"

Dan Gorbunow, AMT, is a healer, educator, and public speaker. Dan's life and mission have been shaped by decades of practice in traditional Eastern medicine, martial arts, and spirituality.

Connect with Dan:
Integral health courses and retreats help you repair energy, spirit, and mind through a holistic philosophy and ancient medicine. Check out Dan's introduction to the art and methods of sacred wellness at: www.WarriorVox.com/SacredWellness

Shift your pattern and access your inner gold through Dan's online course Healing the Father Archetype: Reclaim Your Vitality and Success, available at: www.transformationschool/healingthefather.com

Enjoy a deep dive into personal work, mission, and service in his spirit-based addiction recovery programs at: www.SevenFeathersSociety.org

Dan's book about men's healing, The Dying and Reborn Man, due for publication in December 2022, is available for pre-order at: www.WarriorVox.com/Publications

To inquire about Dan's offerings or for wellness consultation, including appointments for healing sessions using Traditional Chinese Medicine, holistic bodywork, ancestral reconciliation, and spiritual repair, email him at WarriorVox@gmail.com

Dan also enjoys cooking, travel, design, wildcrafting, dance, film, storytelling, and creating learning adventures for his family, friends, and clients.

CHAPTER 5

BECOMING THE MAN MY CHILDREN WOULD WANT TO KNOW

Jere Friedman, J.D., M.A., CMMI

David (not his real name) looked as if I had hit him between the eyes with a two-by-four. I had asked a simple yet profound question. It was a question that would change the course of his life forever.

David and I were having lunch at an upscale restaurant in the financial district of Phoenix, Arizona. David said, "I'm miserable. My marriage is intolerable." He described his wife's raging anger at him, their power struggles over whether their children should go to church with him, and the utter dysfunctionality of their relationship. "My attorney is preparing divorce papers," he said, "but nothing has been filed yet."

David also shared how he'd been looking at pornography and, occasionally, visiting prostitutes. "I've been exploring internet dating," he said. "I've met a woman online who is very interesting. I've had some online conversations with her, and I'm thinking of inviting her to meet me for coffee."

It was then that I leaned forward, looked David in the eyes, and asked softly, "And what is your intention in inviting this woman for coffee?"

I purposefully emphasized the word intention, and the question stopped David in his tracks. I had guessed—correctly—that David had no conscious awareness of his true intention for meeting with the woman. How did I know? Because, like David, there once was a time when I went from one relationship to the next as if sleepwalking, without looking at what I was doing, who I was choosing as a partner, or why. For many years, my intimate relationships with women were based primarily on satisfying my sexual needs and my desire for someone who would mother me. My involvement in these relationships was shallow, selfish, and immature. Like David, at one time I was a very hot mess.

Learning to live life with intentionality was just one of many steps in my transcendence from the muck and mire to an awareness of the joy, beauty, and fulfillment that is our natural birthright. And I'm proud of how I'm now able to share my story, life experience, and skills as a coach, healer, teacher, guide, and minister as I support others on their life journey.

But, I did not always have those skills and experience.

I was 28 years old when I finally faced some harsh realities. *I'm broke,* I reflected. *I'm about to be divorced, and I have two very young children. I've squandered away a small inheritance, and I'm not earning enough to support myself, much less a soon-to-be ex-wife and a young son and daughter.* I was severely depressed and was using alcohol and marijuana to numb my anguish and my dissatisfaction, discomfort, and rejection of myself (my Self) and my responsibilities. *My life is an absolute shambles,* I admitted to myself.

I awoke to a painful reality. *Nothing is working—what I believe about myself, how I think I should live my life or the way I think things should be. I need to step back, start over, and learn a new way of navigating through life—a new way of being.* Thus began my journey of transcendence to how I experience life today.

I moved back in with my parents. At age 30 and working full-time in the family-owned commercial real estate business, I enrolled in a local university to complete my undergraduate degree. My life was finally turning around. Although I was still drinking almost daily and smoking weed to numb my inner unhappiness, for the most part I was functioning in ways that our general culture would consider to be mature and acceptable. Best of all, each visit with my children was better than the last as I accepted the reality that I was a parent and capable of fulfilling that role. My kids and I were having more fun and sharing greater love and connection in our times together.

And then the bottom fell out. Through circumstances beyond my control, it became impossible for me to be with my children for an indefinite period of time. *This isn't fair!* I screamed to myself. *I don't deserve this! But most of all, it's not fair to the kids! They should know my family and me as they grow up. That's what would be in their best interest.*

For two years, I did everything I could think of to change the situation. I was confused, hurt, and angry but kept my rage bottled up inside me until I developed an ulcer. I spent thousands of dollars on attorneys who eventually said they could do nothing for me. Ultimately, I conceded that there was nothing more that I could do. Utterly heartbroken, I thought, *Okay then, I'll let my ex-wife and kids get on with their lives, and I'll get on with mine. But God, if you're listening, I make this solemn commitment to you: I will do whatever I have to do to become the man my children would want to know as their father. And I hope and pray that one day they will be willing to give me a chance and see that I'm a pretty good guy after all.*

I completed my undergrad program and graduated with a bachelor's degree at age 32. I continued working in the family real estate business and stopped smoking weed. A few years later, I went on to law school, where I studied hard and did well. I saw how my almost daily drinking was getting in my way, so I stopped drinking. I graduated with honors and landed a job at a prestigious law firm in Phoenix, Arizona. My work was challenging and yet rewarding. *I'm really on my way now,* I thought.

Yet, my intimate relationships with women remained out of kilter. Following an intense, chaotic, and volatile fling while in law school, I finally took a look at what I'd been doing, what I was and wasn't seeking, and the women I'd been choosing to sleep with. *This clearly isn't working,* I thought. *Perhaps I should try something different.*

Growth, change, and transformation require us to get out of our comfort zone. *If I want to create different results, I'll have to get out of the comfort zone of how I've always done things in the past to open a path for healing old wounds and choosing a new way of being in my life.*

Soon after moving to Phoenix, I began six years of intense psychoanalysis. Several years later, I earned a master's degree in Spiritual Psychology from the University of Santa Monica (USM). Spiritual Psychology engages us in exploring the evolution of human consciousness. It helps us answer the questions, "Who am I? Why am I here? And, how can I make a meaningful difference in the world?"

At USM, I learned and integrated concepts and practices that truly have transformed my day-to-day, moment-to-moment life experience. I once saw my life through the lens of being a victim of outside people and circumstances. I have rewritten my life story, and I now see myself as a hero who has overcome great challenges and who now celebrates the beauty of the world and enjoys the abundance that is always available to each of us. Following are a few examples of practices I learned at USM and that now support me on my journey through life:

- Seeing the loving essence in myself and others. When I see myself and others as Divine beings having a human experience, I open to the reality that our true nature is love. I relate to myself and others from a center of love and compassion instead of fear and insecurity. I remember that we are all doing the best we can at all times. I now understand that if we could do better, we would.

- Heart-centered listening enables me to pay attention and listen to the deeper meaning beyond the plain words that the other person is saying. Perhaps this person is hurt or afraid of being hurt in some way, I think. Perhaps they are insecure or unsure of how to take the next step in their life. By really listening to another person, I may cultivate a deeper understanding of them and what they're struggling with, which facilitates compassion and creates greater trust and connection in our relationship.

- Using everything for learning, growth, and healing. At USM, we learned that "Planet Earth is a school, and everyone has a unique curriculum to complete." The challenges and upsets we encounter along the way are there to help us learn, grow, and heal. Over time I was able to see that my separation from my children was an opportunity to examine what led up to that situation and choose a different course in my life from that time forward. Painful though it was, that separation ultimately was a great gift to my family and me.

- The power of positive intention. I learned that blindly going through life leads to a life without meaning or purpose and, potentially, disastrous results like the separation from my children. On the other hand, I have experienced how having a clear, positive intention opens the door to infinite possibilities in my life. When I slow down and consciously articulate my intention about a course of action, I invite the Universe to complete the scene in ways that are far more beautiful and creative than anything that I might imagine.

That deep inner work helped me gain insight into who I really am and the family and other dynamics that led me to make the choices that I'd been making previously, choices that were harmful to me as well as to others. It also helped me see that I could make different choices—healthy choices—not based on the false beliefs about myself and the world I learned from my parents, at school, or from Madison Avenue.

For example, I grew up in the Deep South in the 1950s and 1960s. I witnessed cultural norms based on what I now see as domination, oppression, and humiliation of others based on the color of their skin or gender. And although I objected to those norms and spoke out against them, in certain ways I also unconsciously adopted those norms and engaged in behaviors that objectified or demeaned others—particularly women. Once I became aware of these behaviors, I could choose to act differently.

While at USM, I participated in a men's group that met monthly. A profoundly different energy and conversation emerge when men gather in a safe environment where only other men are present. It was extremely valuable and supportive for me to hear other men's stories, concerns, doubts, hopes, fears, and accomplishments and to be able to share my own. We opened up, allowed ourselves to become vulnerable, and expressed things that were on our hearts but that we otherwise kept locked deep inside—things that, as boys, we learned it was *not* okay to share.

Like most other men, I learned at an early age that we will be judged as "weak" if we feel, much less express, our fears, concerns, and insecurities. I still cringe and squirm whenever I remember one particularly dreadful moment. I was a terrified first grader on the drill field at an all-boys military day school. An upperclassman was reprimanding me for something, and I burst out in tears. Enraged, he leaned in until he was only inches from my face and screamed, "Don't cry!" His own face became beet red as he drove home the final nail, "Boys, don't cry!" I stifled the hurt, and it was many years later before I once again allowed myself to indulge in the healing release of a good cry.

As I continued my participation in the men's group, I heaved a sigh of relief as I realized *I am not alone in my struggles and insecurities. I'm not the only little boy going through life in the body of an adult male but bearing the wounds of my childhood. And although the sources of our wounds are unique to each man, there is a common theme that runs through our collective stories. I have something in common with each of these other men. We have been shamed, humiliated, and told that we are unworthy of love or not good enough in some way. I'm not the only one who grew up in a household where love is conditional. Sadly, we have all been beaten, molested, or abandoned in some way—physically, emotionally, psychologically, or all of the above.*

And yet, by opening up and becoming vulnerable, sharing my stories, and reaching out and touching other men in the group—with my words, heart, or hands—I learned I could and do help others heal as I heal myself. *I'm not helpless!* I exclaimed to myself one day. *I am helpful! I can safely let go of my old stories, in which I am the victim, and write a new story for myself.*

In my new story, I am strong, courageous, wise, kind, gentle, and loving. In my new story, I give myself permission to experience all my emotions— joy, sorrow, anger, love—without shame and without fear that I will die (in a figurative sense) if I go there. In my new story, I am not broken. Instead, I am good enough.

I became intrigued by some new questions as I witnessed my own growth and healing and that of the other men in the group. *We are smart, sensitive, well-intentioned men. We've come of age during the rise of women's liberation and the feminist movement. We know, or think we know, what we should not say, do, or touch. But too often, we seem lost when it comes to taking our rightful place as partners, brothers, fathers, sons, or leaders in our community.*

I began to explore a number of interesting and challenging questions about myself. *Who am I as a man? What is masculinity, and how do I express that power in a positive, constructive, and loving manner? How can I more fully show up as a man for myself, my wife and children, and my community?*

This exploration is still very much a work in process. My answer so far has been that *I am a <u>true</u> man who is kind, honest, and loving, a man who keeps his word, and a man who lives a life of integrity in which I am helpful to myself, my loved ones, my community, and all of Planet Earth.*

I believe it's time for men to step up, do their inner work, and step boldly into an awareness of our inherent strength and magnificence as Divine beings currently in a male body. It's time for us to serve ourselves, our partners, and the world as authentic men. This belief inspired me to create the Authentic Man Project as a vehicle to continue my own growth and expansion and a means by which I support other men, including David, in transforming their lives. I find meaning, fulfillment, and purpose in my life as I share my stories, my journey, and my experience with fellow men who are ready to unlearn old, unhealthy beliefs and patterns, step out of self-destructive behaviors and dysfunctional relationships and replace them with a positive self-image, inner peace, fulfillment, and healthy relationships.

The journey that began at age 28—now 40 years ago—continues. I may have mastered skills to a certain extent and gained some insight into the questions described above, yet I remain a work-in-progress and will be just that for the remainder of my life. At the same time, I now experience profound joy, satisfaction, and fulfillment whenever I have the opportunity to use my skills and experience to support others—men and women—on their own journeys of transformation and transcendence.

One more key ingredient in my transformation was meeting Ellen shortly after I moved to Phoenix. Ellen is unlike any of the women that I'd previously chosen as a mate. Heck, Ellen is unlike any other woman, period! We've created a wonderful relationship for over 28 years now. We are friends, lovers, and partners. We make an effort to communicate well and lovingly. We're grateful for one another, and we don't take each other for granted.

Ellen supported me in reaching out to my son and daughter after a 20-year separation. Thankfully, they welcomed the opportunity to reconnect. We've enjoyed a wonderful, close, and loving relationship over the last 18 years, and we just keep getting closer and closer. Best of all, this connection has added two beautiful granddaughters to Ellen and my lives!

I've enjoyed many successes over the years, but my transcendence to become the man my children would want to know as their father is by far my greatest success story.

I leave you with this thought: If I can do it, you can do it! *You* can transform your life, transcend whatever challenges you face and, with

Spirit's guidance and support, manifest what your heart desires. In my work as a coach, healer, minister, and guide, I've found that each of us already has the answers we seek. We just need the right question.

I would welcome the opportunity to speak with you and explore whether and how I might be able to support you on your magnificent journey. Perhaps I'll have just the right question for you, as I've had for David and many others!

May you be blessed always, and in all ways.

Jere Friedman, J.D., M.A., CMMI, is an employee of the Universe—*with full benefits!* Jere holds a master's degree in Spiritual Psychology and uses that training, along with other skills and life experience, in his work as a soul-centered coach, gongmaster, certified meditation and mindfulness instructor, certified breathwork healer, minister, and practicing attorney.

Jere's life work is to contribute to the evolution of consciousness on Planet Earth by supporting others in finding their own way to joy, fulfillment, and inner peace. Jere is available for one-on-one and group coaching. He also facilitates classes, workshops, and retreats and does public speaking for the general public as well as in professional and corporate settings. Topics include spirituality, Spiritual Psychology, meditation and mindfulness, conscious leadership, reclaiming your life from burnout, and many others. Jere also leads The Authentic Man Project, which consists of various programs, mastermind groups, weekend retreats, and group or one-on-one coaching designed to create a safe environment in which men can learn and integrate more authentic ways of expressing their masculinity in today's world.

Jere also regularly facilitates public and private gongbaths and sound healing sessions, Gong and Breathwork Healing Journeys, and Cacao and Gongbath Ceremonies. Playing gongs allows Jere's Inner Child to come out to play and teaches him to be present and focused in the moment.

Jere has personally experienced the transformational rewards of reduced stress, increased inner peace and calm, enhanced relationships, improved focus and efficiency, heightened intuition, and living a more authentic life that becomes available when a person makes a commitment to himself or herself to reclaim his or her birthright. Ask Jere—he'll show you how easy it is to claim these benefits for yourself!

Please visit www.jerefriedman.com and www.gong2heaven.com for more information. Contact Jere at info@jerefriedman.com

CHAPTER 6

SEEKING THE PIECES TO BE A WHOLE MAN

JOURNEY TO SOUL PURPOSE

Rev Will Halm, Reiki Master

I'm at the past life workshop on the last day. A participant came in and started to share with the group for the first time. She avoided any opportunities to share prior to this moment. "I've come to clear any blocks or distortions getting in my way of becoming an animal communicator." Still damp from a morning swim in the ocean with several pods of dolphins, she shared a past life in which she was a seal, was saved by three fishermen, and snuck back in the water by one of the fishermen. Dolphins came and took her to safety. Having swum with the dolphins that morning, she had messages for each person in the training group. Each person was surprised and appreciated what they were told. My message was, "The dolphins want you to live your life with your heart more open." That message led me to name my counseling/reiki practice, DolphinHeartsWay. So how did I get to this place in my life?

My life started in what appeared to be a normal suburban home in a middle-class neighborhood 14 miles outside New York City. The homes were well kept, with yards attended to on a street where there were tall trees shading the houses. From the outside, it looked like it was middle class normal. For me, inside this house, it was far from normal. Some days were simply being on edge listening to how a doorknob was turned or what footsteps sounded like, or the edge in a parent's voice. I was a highly sensitive, empathic boy who wondered if Mr. Hyde or Dr. Jekyll was going to show up that night. There were unwritten rules to follow, such as "don't cry," "don't be angry," and "never let anyone know what goes on here."

The household slid fairly quickly into low-bottom alcoholism, where parenting was gone and figuring out by oneself how to survive took over. It was violent, abusive, and silenced a little boy. By age ten, I had a paper route to make some money, and at age 12, I got a job in a restaurant kitchen washing dishes and pots and pans. The survival wisdom in my head was: *work hard and fast, be perfect, and you'll be okay.* By age 14, I was making money to buy clothes and make sure I could eat. I was lonely. I wasn't involved in any teenage peer activities. I worked hard and performed for a compliment from the boss. I was a good kid, and I was carrying around the atrocities of the alcoholic home.

Also, at age 14, I found the magic elixir—alcohol, and it numbed the pain and fear I carried. *For some moments in the evening, I would ponder what my place in this world was. Drinking gave me the thought that maybe I do belong.* This part of my young life was about getting up each morning, going to school, working 40 hours a week, and having those magical weekend nights where I danced with my new partner, alcohol.

I sailed through high school with good enough grades and no plans after graduation. I had found the magic elixir. Graduation came and went. I was lost in the haze of drinking and doing what I did well—working. This time of living with the survival skill I learned in my home and my dance with substances was rudely interrupted by the invitation from the Selective Service Draft Board to show up for a physical exam. It was an invitation I couldn't avoid or get out of showing up for—induction into the Army.

My experience in the Army started out well as I figured out how to *read the expectations and perform.* I did very well at first until betrayal and abuse occurred within my unit toward me. It triggered the fear, pain, anger, and shame I carried from my childhood and had camouflaged. There was not enough alcohol or other substances that could contain it anymore. After one year, three months, nine days, three hours, and 27 minutes, I was washed out of the Army with a general discharge and the message, "You will never amount to anything." For the next seven years, my life was like an old jalopy on a country road, rattling and threatening to fall apart. I lived and traveled in 35 different states and had 43 different kinds of jobs.

I finally landed in a recovery program where I awakened to the realization there was more to life than the shame-based, fear-encrusted, angry explosions I was living. The surrender did not come easily. I had quite a victim consciousness, and I was learning the lesson of taking responsibility for my life. A man named Frank shook his head and said, "You're quite a piece of work." Besides Frank's message, I heard people's stories of growth, hope, and transformation. I was hungry for that. I witnessed people having a connection to spirituality. I wanted that also. I immersed myself in the program. I tried to go into religion, and that didn't seem to connect me to the peace, serenity, and productive lives I saw in the recovery people. I was active in surrender, self-awareness, and service.

With my life transforming and experiencing some connection, a woman paid attention to me and laughed at my humor; I knew she was the one. Thus began my seeking relationships, emotional intimacy, and marriage. I was way behind in this area and had the desire to find it. As one might guess, this required more action on my part. Sitting with my sponsor, he would help me see what I needed to let go of, helped me awaken to self-awareness, and how to take better action in service to the world. He said, "This is a journey, not a sudden event." It took two major relationships and three marriages to find a heart partner. It was a new level of seeking and learning. There was a new language of feelings to learn and to become literate in: mad, sad, glad, scared, etc. And a whole lot of gradations of them. Relationships took me into classes on commitment, honesty, responsibility, boundaries, sensuality, and sexuality. The main course in my family of origin was survival, so this school of relationships had many lessons to teach me.

While I was living with curiosity and seeking spirituality, I had the good fortune to attend a men's retreat with three indigenous men and a man who spent 15 years with the aborigines of the Outback. They led and taught through storytelling and simply by their presence on topics of spirituality, right relationship, grief, and nature. It was as if I was immersed in an ocean of wisdom, and every cell of my being was drinking it in. As I walked away from that retreat, I heard myself say, "Life is not gonna be the same." My eyes were opened to how much healing I had to do and how much more there was to learn in so many areas.

The deeper journey started with a three-year training in Unergi, a body psychotherapy that blended together with a number of modalities creating emotional and sensory intelligence and beginning a clearing and healing of deep sexual abuse and other traumas. As a result of this work and exploration, my sense of self—how I engaged the world around me—changed. I was not the same person. People noticed and told me, "You're not the same person." I also had a similar experience after attending a dance, movement, and energy workshop.

At this time, I was facilitating a residential experiential program to help people address deep issues from their family of origin. I witnessed and experienced a deeper level of emotional and energetic awareness working with these clients. My daily experience was exposure to a group of people's trauma and abuse. This activated a secondary PTSD for me. I found myself anxious and somewhat compulsive. In seeking relief from that, I was attuned to Usui Reiki which began a self-care practice to deal with the anxiety. It was an effective technique to calm me, and it increased the sensitivity I had toward the people I worked with. I've since been attuned to a variety of lineages of Reiki and other healing energies.

The desire to seek a stronger spiritual connection led me to an introductory workshop on Shamanic Journeying. Traveling to a non-ordinary reality elevated me to a calm awareness like no other and led me, for a while, to also participate in sweat lodges, which for me was a time for prayer. Also, I would sit on a jetty at the ocean's edge and send Reiki to the dolphins. Once I started to send the Reiki, they would come. Humans who wanted a close-up experience with the dolphins came too. Sometimes I would get a boogie board and float in the water, and the dolphins would swim around me. I found gentleness, playfulness, and kindness were concepts I wanted to have more of in my life.

This all made me more aware and sensitive to energies and emotions as the inner empath awakened. Sometimes friends, or even wives, were uncomfortable with it and left my life. I continued to seek and found more training that seemed to give me more of what I was seeking. I was drawn to several workshops led by Dr. Brian Weiss on past life regression work. He's an Ivy League-trained psychiatrist who used hypnosis to help a person travel back in their consciousness before their grief started. The experience of traveling further back into other lifetimes is very therapeutic. Dr. Weiss is one of the most patient, generous, loving human beings I have met in my life.

Another training I was involved in was something called Soul Retrieval. This shamanic technique allows the practitioner to travel into non-ordinary reality to retrieve soul fragments lost by traumatic events. This work was astounding to receive and also facilitate. It restored aspects of people that held lost qualities of themselves. To witness a person changing and becoming more has been so rewarding.

During this time, I was feeling a distance in my relationship with my grown children. Contact with my son was broken for months at a time, and my daughter would say, "It's okay," even when it wasn't. I got involved in something called Family Constellation work. In learning and practicing Constellation work, it positively affected my relationship with my grown children. The work itself is about addressing the energy field of your lineage or genogram. When certain things are addressed, the energy of your field changes, and it can affect your current life experiences. In my situation, six of the seven generations of my father's lineage have all had military experiences that impacted their lives.

I have mentioned all these training experiences because, over time, they've helped me evolve from a very immature, self-centered individual to more of a conscious man involved in helping people step into the best version of themselves. More than 45 years ago, I prayed from a seclusion room in a psychiatric ward of a VA hospital—a plea to God I didn't believe in at that time: "If you help me, God, I will dedicate my life to helping people."

It happened, and I did, and I am grateful. I've been gifted with being able to witness God's answer to that prayer so long ago. I've seen a 43-year-old minister come to a prayer group asking for prayers to heal cancer: "I have two small children and a calling that is not complete." We prayed, and he let the group know that after that night, the doctors could find no evidence of cancer. A woman and her husband sought help to heal whatever was preventing them from having children for ten years. We did some energy work, and the next month she was pregnant. There are many more examples of the Divine's answer to my plea; I'm 43 years sober and have witnessed so much healing, growth, and transformation.

In my search, I discovered many things. I discovered the world was not 100% cold and heartless. There is kindness, compassion, and love. As a teenager, I pursued a course to escape pain and was unaware that I was creating more. When I reached sobriety, a whole new world unfolded. I discovered that emotional safety could be found in one's self. Not only was there emotional safety, there was guidance from emotional literacy. For instance, anger could be giving a message that something has intruded or is wrong. Sadness can inform us when something is gone, leaving, or was needed and never there. Joy can show us an adventure in dreams and positive experiences. Fear can be a warning that there is danger. In general, our feelings can give us feedback about our life's journey.

In searching for healing, I found I could create a healing container for myself. The healing container has components anyone can develop. I have called them the four Ss. Here they are around the container. The first side of the container is Support. This is best described as an "A-team" of several people that love, support, and encourage you without harsh judgment. The next side of this container is Spirituality. Spirituality, in this case, is a personal practice that in some way connects you to the greater whole. Some people find this in religion or in nature by hugging a tree or growing a garden. The next S is Self-Care. This is the development of practices on an emotional, physical, and mental level that soothe, calm, empower, or develop one in healthy ways. The last side of this container is Strengths. This entails making an inventory of personal strengths such as compassion, honesty, responsibility, etc. In such a personal container, a person can develop an awareness and ability to address their issues and make changes to their life.

All these discoveries from my seeking have helped the man who grew up silenced by abuse and trauma to find a voice. This voice has been used along the way to help people find their voice. It has helped to be able to speak about needs, desires, and boundaries. As a highly sensitive person and empath, it was hard to navigate the world. I would pick up someone's mood, emotion, attitude, or physical sensations, such as a headache. At times in my life, that was overwhelming. I've learned to question myself: *Is this energy mine or yours?* It feels like more of a gift now that I've found some answers about being highly sensitive and an empath.

I've come a long way from that silenced little boy to the man I am today. The voice I have found and shared is about kindness, compassion, love, encouragement, and the lack of judgment. It has never been about better-than, smarter-than, etc. It is usually about expressing some sort of message like, "How may I serve?" or "What would love do here?"

Will Halm is a mystic and a seeker. He describes his path to be a holder of sacred space for people to step into the best version of themselves. In his early years, he was challenged with many difficulties from traumas and addiction. Upon awakening spiritually, Will has pursued many interests for himself. In all that he embraced, he passed on to others. Originally trained as an addictions counselor and ordained as a minister in the Sanctuary of the Beloved. His ongoing interests include Family Sculpturing, Reiki, Shamanic practices including Soul Retrieval, and Past Life Regressions. Will's ongoing passion is in Psychodrama, where people can have an embodied experience of change and healing. Will enjoys life with his heart partner and fur baby on the shore of a small cove in central Maryland. Will can be engaged via email at dolphinsway7@aol.com

CHAPTER 7

UNMASK YOUR SOUL

FIND PEACE WITHIN

Saahil Mehta

Anyone looking at the car crash would have surely thought the chances of survival were slim. It wasn't our time to go yet. God protected my wife and I as we walked away with just minor bruises.

The first thing I pushed aside as I was growing my business was my relationships, and the second was my health.

It was the summer of 2015, and the sky was already dark as I entered my home exhausted from a very long day at work. Yet again, I missed dinner with the family and tucking the kids to bed. No matter how hard I tried at the game of life, it just wasn't enough. I felt I was on a treadmill, running but going nowhere. I was doing the best I could, but it wasn't working, so I ran faster. The reality of the situation was I was burning out and digging myself an early grave.

I was being pulled in all directions and overwhelmed as there just weren't enough hours in the day.

With the fear of judgment holding me back, I blocked my emotions by saying to myself, *Better to be quiet than get into a confrontation.* I felt very alone on this journey. Emotions are energy in motion, and by blocking them and preventing them from flowing, the energy was stagnant inside of me. Just like stagnant water, the environment in my body became contaminated. And when the energy did find some release, it would often be in the form of sickness or bursts of anger. I would have a short fuse and get angry easily and quickly—usually to the people that matter most in my life.

I didn't even realize when sickness became prominent as it slowly crept in, and rather than addressing it (mainly because the challenges I felt were not big enough to see a doctor but enough to be an irritant in my life), I just accepted them as being a part of me. Little did I realize the imbalance in my mind was causing an imbalance in my body too. I was constantly bloated, which I later realized was due to inflammation, which caused all sorts of issues with my gut. In addition, I experienced energy dips which at times would be so bad that I found it hard to stay awake. I have fallen asleep in a restaurant, a nightclub, and on the sofa while engaging with friends, but worst of all was when I fell asleep behind the wheel, which almost cost the life of my wife, Ekta, and of course, myself.

Although I accepted all this as being a part of me, the reality is that if something doesn't feel right, it probably isn't.

2016, The Year I Woke Up!

In the spring of 2016, I was on my way to the island of Ibiza with members of my forum from the Entrepreneurs Organization (EO), a global organization of entrepreneurs that helps you achieve your full potential in your business and personal life through life-enhancing connections, shared experiences, and collaborative learning. While waiting at the gate of Barcelona airport, I turned to Vinny and asked, "How can we make this trip more magical?"

We agreed to two words which we shared with the rest of the group, and those were *"no judgment."* All of a sudden, a huge weight was lifted off my shoulders; I didn't have to pretend to be someone I wasn't, I didn't have to be a people pleaser, and I could just be me.

The next four days were euphoric and filled with joy. We were dining at Lio one evening, a restaurant with entertainment such as singing, dancing, acrobatics, etc. Our table was situated right next to the stage, and I happened to be sitting closest to it. During the last act, one of the dancers pointed to me and gave the signal to come up. The previous me, a man who fears judgment, would've shrunk back in my chair and looked the other way or would have pretended to be on my phone, even though I love to dance.

With no fear of judgment, I took the opportunity and experienced a feeling of liberation. The remainder of the trip was filled with similar experiences where I felt freer.

On the flight on my way back home, I wanted to share these moments with Ekta, so I started to journal. During this process, tears started to trickle down my face as I felt overwhelmed by the whole experience. What was happening? Prior to this, it was very rare for me to cry as I saw the vulnerability as a sign of weakness. Here, however, in this safe space of no judgment, I couldn't stop crying for what seemed like hours. I realized I had commenced on my path to finding my purpose and discovering who I really am. Through a higher level of awareness, I understood that I became vulnerable by removing my masks and becoming my authentic, true self. I couldn't recall the last time I felt this way for so many days.

How long had I been hiding behind these masks? How many masks was I wearing?

By trying to make everyone else happy, I only found emptiness and unhappiness. I knew I didn't want to go back to the man I used to be, a man who feared judgment. This fear added clutter to all areas of my life.

Growing up in the quaint town of Wilrijk on the outskirts of Antwerp in Belgium and being raised by two amazing souls was the best childhood I could've ever asked for. The country was safe and green, filled with humble people who were always willing to help. My father sacrificed family time for work in order to earn more so my sister and I would get the best education, travel the world, and have material possessions he could only dream of. This was his way of showing love. My mother sacrificed her time and was a housewife to ensure we were given all the support we needed in all areas of our lives and was there for us through thick and thin—she made us her number one priority, which was her way of showing love. I could not have asked for better parents.

Even with all that love, I felt somewhat lost. Rather than trying to find myself, I tried to fit in. I was doing things to make others happy regardless of how it made me feel. Instead of addressing the various challenges at the core, I just allowed more and more layers of clutter to cloud me, taking me further away from my true self.

But eventually, after peeling through the layers, I started to identify the sources which led to the blocked emotions:

1. Communication with my parents was usually one-way. They instructed, and I followed. This was the way they were brought up and was the way they knew how to parent.

2. My father would shower little praise for my successes. In his mind, that would make me weak, and he wanted me to be strong.

3. I grew up in an environment where men were tough and took care of the family—vulnerability was a sign of weakness.

4. My father loved his work; it was in his blood. From the perspective of a child, however, I would not see him on sports days or school performances. That amplified when I had two older cousins stay with us for several years who were in the same workplace. Work started coming home, and the father/son time became even less.

For all the reasons above, I created a wall around me to protect myself from the outside. Little did I know, this also prevented me from expressing myself and enjoying the beauty that is life.

From my perspective, however, life was great, and I was just facing various challenges like everyone else. My journey in Ibiza made me realize how beautiful life could really be. Imagine walking your whole life barefoot, and one day someone was to offer you the most comfortable shoes, allowing each journey to be a miracle. That is what I experienced. Even though I live in a world filled with judgment, even if I could be half the man I was during that fortuitous trip, I would be much better off than I was.

Upon my return to Dubai, the first thing I did was make myself my number one priority. Only if *my* cup was overflowing would I have enough energy to impact others and live the life I was born for. I started to identify what was preventing me from being my true authentic self.

What confrontations was I shunning?

I eventually called all this clutter—essentially anything that no longer served any function or purpose in my life.

I opened up with friends about my health challenges and was directed to an integrative functional doctor who helped me discover my intolerances and vitamin deficiencies (which later I would discover were primarily due to my mental health). As soon as I stopped eating the food that was harming my body and supplemented what was lacking, my body went through an amazing transformation. I lost ten percent of my body weight, which was pretty much all fat, as a result of the inflammation almost disappearing. I rarely had energy dips anymore, allowing for a much higher level of productivity. If I could achieve so much after decluttering my body, imagine what I could achieve from decluttering other areas of my life.

What next?

Since our first climb in December 2010 to Kala Patthar, a little higher than the base of Mount Everest at 18,192ft, Ekta and I said to one another, "That was amazing! We must climb another mountain soon." Years passed, and I always found a reason not to go, whether it was work, family, or the many other excuses I made. It was the summer of 2016, and our children were old enough to stay with their grandparents. It was time to conquer ourselves again. As Sir Edmund Hillary said, "It's not the mountain we conquer, but ourselves." So I booked to climb Kilimanjaro in January 2017. The mountains have been calling me for years, and it was time to fuel that passion again and continue to climb the world's tallest mountains—no more excuses.

One evening over dinner with my fellow climbers, I asked them, "What do you miss the most?" Without hesitation, they all said, "kids." Hilarious how none were missing their husbands. I asked again and made it clear to exclude people. They all came back with the following three things: a warm room, a bed, and running water. That's when it struck me, I keep saying, "I need this, and I need that," but in reality, I have everything I need—food, shelter, basic clothing, and you may even argue, the internet. Everything else is a want or desire. I started to go through most of my belongings and started to give things away. I felt lighter as there were fewer things to worry about. In this process, I was also decluttering my mind, which was opening up space for things that truly matter in my life.

After our return from Kilimanjaro, a spiritual teacher (Brahmrishi Guruvanand Ji Maharaj) visited our house to give a talk. Growing up, the only rituals pushed on me were over the understanding of Jainism (the religion I grew up with). Coupled with my engineering mind, which would only believe what could be proven by science, I'd always be very skeptical about such people and anything related to religion. After removing some of the clutter in my life, I came to the realization that the mind belongs to this body which has limited knowledge, whereas the soul is connected to the Divine, which is infinite knowledge.

If that is the case, why am I giving limited knowledge more power?

Just because science cannot explain it today does not mean it will not be explained one day. I started tuning in with my intuition a lot more, which allowed me to receive. I'd slowly find out that the Divine was always answering my questions and showing me the way; I was just too blind to see.

After the fascinating talk, which triggered several big questions about my purpose, detachment, and love, the Guru manifested a gold pendant of a hand with some writing on it and gave it to me. I did not think much of it at the time and put it safely away.

Later that year, in the summer of 2017, we stayed with my in-laws in New Jersey to escape the Dubai heat. As I started reading during my morning ritual, my inner voice said, *Don't read here; go down to the library.* Previously, I would have ignored my inner voice, but now I was curious and played along. Once in the library, my inner voice said, *There is a book that is here for you.* I started to scan the vast library, and one book was staring at my face—*The Jain Way of Life.* This startled me as I was not religious at all. *So why this book?* Once again, I went with my inner voice and proceeded with curiosity. To my surprise, I came across the image of the same hand the guru gave me just a few months back! I read the meaning, which was to stop and reflect rather than be constantly running. Inside the hand was just one word, "Ahimsa," which is Sanskrit for non-violence.

In an instant, it became clear to me that my purpose in life is to live, breathe, and spread the non-violent way of living. This journey I was on to declutter my life was bringing peace within. Peace within results in more peace on the outside which will bring peace to the world. My mission is to help people eradicate the clutter in their life so they too can find peace within as we move towards a world of greater peace and higher consciousness.

I was moving at a very fast pace. With each round of decluttering my mind, body, relationships, and the material world, I was clearer, and life kept getting better. Even with all the highs, I was becoming aware of two important relationships that had started to become distant: Ekta and my father. I chose to focus my energies first on my number two priority (number one being myself, of course), Ekta.

I couldn't pinpoint what it could be, as no one had done anything which would be deemed unethical; however, we felt disconnected. I still recall the conversation where she turned to me and said, "Saahil, I don't recognize you anymore. You're not the man I married."

I was changing at such a rapid pace; how could she keep up? Coupled with a lot of our time going towards our young kids and various obligations, we rarely brought up the topic. When we did, however, the conversation wouldn't go well, from my side at least. I chose to avoid it, hoping it would go away or things would magically get better. The reality was that it only got worse; something had to change. I realized the only way to bridge the gap was through communication by creating a safe space where we could open up without being judged, which is what we did.

During my 40th birthday celebration on a spiritual journey in Bali in December 2019, I received a phone call from my father, "Saahil, you must have received an OTP on your phone; please, can you share it with me." We hadn't spoken for days, and that was the depth of our conversation. Even though our relationship had become distant, my intuition was shouting at me, *What is going on? Is your relationship only transactional? Where is the love?*

I picked up the phone and called him back. "Dad, I'm just calling you to tell you I love you." In an instant, we both broke down into tears. It was a beautiful moment. I realized then that I had to take the necessary steps to build the father/son relationship and fill it with love.

Upon my return, we spent several moments together opening up and sharing our perspectives. There was laughter, tears, disagreements, and more. The end result was higher respect for one another and, more importantly, a greater level of love. I am so blessed to have had those special moments with my father because on March 13th, 2021, his soul departed his body. Wherever the soul is today, our bond is stronger than ever before.

During this whole time, I came to one big realization that we are all beautiful souls who are children of God. The more I have decluttered my life (and continue to do so), the more I'm in love with God, myself, Gaia, and all those around me. I look at each challenge with curiosity and focus on learning rather than playing the victim. I'm a soul on a path of liberation, and it's my duty to my fellow souls to support them on their journey.

I now live life with greater awareness.
I now live life with more energy.
I now live life with stronger relationships.
I now live life.

Saahil Mehta

saahil@saahilmehta.com

www.saahilmehta.com

https://www.instagram.com/saahilmehtaofficial/

There is nothing more paralyzing than feeling that no matter how hard you work, it's not enough; how much you try to be there for your family, it never works; and no matter how hard you wish to grow healthier, there is always something missing. This is clutter—shunned confrontations—because of which you are always playing catch up with all sorts of clutter in your life.

Saahil's story begins with a similar backdrop. From overcoming the primal human fear of judgment and breaking free from self-imposed limits to living his dream of scaling the world's tallest mountains, Saahil Mehta is the quintessential global entrepreneur turned advocate of the power of decluttering your life.

As a global citizen, Saahil has built successful businesses across three continents, but he struggled to experience peace, happiness, and abundance even thereafter. And only once he conquered his self-limiting mental, emotional and physical clutter was he able to re-invent the 4-key dimensions of his life. With his debut book *BREAK-FREE*, he shares his personal journey of how he transcended all odds to scale the summits of his dreams and how you, too, can dream up new personal summits every day once you have mastered the art of decluttering life by adopting his fool-proof process of breaking-free.

Since 2010, Saahil has scaled five of the tallest mountains in the world—a dream he harbored since childhood—and continues living his passion for mountaineering! Today, Saahil has partnered with the legendary Marshall Goldsmith to help ambitious leaders learn the Art of Stakeholder Centered Leadership (SCL). As the Regional Director for the SCL Trainer program for India and the Middle East, Saahil is working towards redefining the Art of Personal and Corporate Leadership to help people scale their summits of success faster.

CHAPTER 8

MISSISSIPPI MUD

A LESSON IN DISCERNMENT

Ken Shepardson

"I'm going away, and I'm never coming back," I declared to my mom and brother over an online voice chat program. We played computer games every night online. Things were changing for me, though I wasn't the man I used to be. I worked in building automation, working on a lot of construction sites. I loved football, smoking pot, and gaming.

2016 is when I started my spiritual journey—it's when I spent some time in the hospital with pancreatitis. When I recovered, I began feeling spirits walking on my bed at night. August of 2020 is when it really started getting interesting for me. After I participated in an online meditation, I felt my third eye crack open, and my clairaudience turned on. Then when I added marijuana, I had some amazing spiritual experiences, which included a kundalini awakening. At the time, I didn't know that's what it was, and as a result, I missed work from kundalini sickness. Afterward, I felt guided to quit my job entirely. *The universe would provide!*

I had been doing research, trying to understand what was going on with me. "I'm a Starseed," I told my family on my birthday that year, being open about my spiritual awakening. One day I heard voices in my head pressuring me to tell my family that I was leaving and was never coming back. I was going to go through some portal and was going to help Earth and humanity on a counsel in space. I have a supportive family, and they had a lot of questions. I did my best to explain, but I didn't understand myself. My mom was in tears for me; we hugged that night. The next morning, I was up early, and that's when I left.

In a pair of shorts, sandals, and a t-shirt, I left Florida on a brisk November morning, leaving everything behind. I started driving north, I didn't know where I was going, but I felt drawn to Utah. Utah called out to me quite a bit during my awakening. I heard spirit say, *They'll track you on the expressways,* so I took side roads. As I reached Georgia, I realized I should have prepared better as it was rather cold. I wound up buying a sweatshirt in a town called Evergreen; the sweatshirt stated it was the Bigfoot capital of Alabama.

The evil voices in my head were telling me, *You're being tracked on your phone,* so I tossed it out the window while driving. On the first day, I made it to Mississippi, every turn and stop guided by spirit. It was night, and I was guided to turn on a road that turned into a dirt road near the Mississippi River. I started to question things at this point, but spirit assured me, *You're on the right track.* Later down that road, I wound up getting stuck in the mud.

I drive a light blue Chevy Volt, and I call her Vickie. I got out of Vickie wearing my shorts and sandals into almost knee-high mud, and it was cold. I walked around her to see if I could get out on my own. Nope, she's stuck. Vickie is equipped with OnStar, so I called them to come to get me out of the mud. Then I leaned the back of the passenger front seat back and brought the back of the back seat forward, creating a bit of a teepee in the car to keep me warm. This is where I slept for the night, covered in mud and freezing.

I woke up the next day at seven in the morning, and OnStar never came. I called them again but figured they wouldn't find me, and I started walking. It was about noon when I made it to some sort of civilization, a camping resort with a little store. I was hungry and thirsty and bought some crackers and Gatorade. I told the people in the store what happened to me and asked for help. A guy who worked at the resort called a friend. While I waited, they gave me some pizza. I'm convinced these people were angels, and I was meant to meet them.

When the friend arrived, the three of us headed out to Vickie in his big 4x4 truck. When they saw how far down the road Vickie was, their jaws dropped in shock. To get the chain around the back tire to pull Vickie out,

I had to pretty much swim in the mud. They tried a few times to pull Vickie out, but she wasn't budging. We paused to look over the situation, and we thought we needed another truck. They decided to give it one more try and were able to pull her out. I was so thankful; Vickie was brown, covered with mud. The guys let me go first to make sure I didn't get stuck again. But I raced out ahead, plowing through any of the rough and rugged terrains as I did the night before. One day I plan to return and tell those people how thankful I am. They are angels!

Back on the road, I decided to start using expressways. Now I was questioning who I heard in my head. I went straight to I-10 and continued west. I made it to Houston and was low on funds. Vickie is a hybrid car; I looked for an outlet in the back of a strip mall I could plug into to charge the car while I slept. Behind one strip mall, I ended up finding an open semi-truck trailer with all kinds of clothes on the ground in front of it. I decided to inspect it for things I could use. I found a somewhat clean bed sheet and a pair of shoes. You have no idea how excited I was to get warm! I set up in Vickie for the night and slept.

The next morning, I started heading north. It was in Madisonville, Texas, that I ran out of gas and money. I decided to ask OnStar if they could call my family. I'm close with my cousin Lisa, and she understands me and my spirituality more than other family members. That's who I asked OnStar to call for me. She sent money via Western Union, but I had to wait until the next day to get it. Because of that, she set me up in a hotel for the night. I was ready for a shower and a bed to sleep in!

In the middle of the night, I woke up and asked spirit what I should do. *Pack what you can carry and start walking; an angel will take you the rest of the way.* Trusting this voice, I packed up and started walking. It was cold! Still, in shorts and sandals, around two in the morning, discernment kicked in. I had only walked about three miles, and I said to myself, *I'm not doing this anymore. This isn't my path.*

I went back to the hotel room and heard a different spirit, one who was more reasonable. They said, *Wouldn't it be better to go back home and take care of your house and things instead of dumping that on your family?* I agreed, and the next morning I picked up the money at Western Union and started heading home. I bought a cheap by-the-minute phone and called my family, who were happy to hear from me. The next day, I was back home in Florida, and I began the process of selling my house and purging my belongings.

A couple of weeks go by, and I start hearing some disturbing voices in my head. They were telling me they were going to lock me in a dog cage to eat dog food for the rest of my life.

I believed I needed to start fighting for my life.

These demons didn't win me over on the Mississippi mud run, and I wasn't about to let them torture me or worse. I did have some good voices that helped me lose the demons. When the demons found me, I could feel them burning me inside my heart. I salted windows and doors in my house as a means of defense; I heard *they don't like salt.* Somehow they would get through. I felt I had to keep moving until I lost them or found a safe space.

This went on for a few nights. I stayed one night at my brother's house, but they found me there too. Then I had a very bad night. I was up all night and spent hours in a salt bath because they couldn't get me while I was in there. This is where I heard, You need to go get on a cruise ship when the sun rises. You'll be safe on the saltwater. They had a harder time chasing me during the day. Of course, this all made complete sense to me at the time. Little did I know that during the pandemic, there were no cruises.

When the sun rose, I packed up a bag and headed for the port. I had to move quickly; I was told the ship was leaving soon. On the way, I got pulled over for speeding but was let go on a warning. I got about five miles from the port and ran out of gas. Determined as ever, I jumped out and started hitchhiking. I was picked up before I got about ten steps away from Vickie. They drove me to the port, and sure enough, no cruise ships. I was devastated. I walked along the port trying to figure out what I needed to do next.

I moved the zippers on my gym bag back and forth in order to hear words in the sound. At the time, this was how my clairaudience worked, and it was how I received direction best. I found a restaurant in between the port slots for the cruise ships, so I went in for breakfast. I ordered steak and eggs and sat on the dock over the saltwater.

From here, I saw a freight hauler being loaded with shipping containers. This was my answer, I was going to get on this boat as a deckhand, and things would work out. The only problem was there were about 50 feet of water between the boat and me. The restaurant was accessible by water, though, and fishermen were lined up. It took a few tries, but I found one willing to take me. He brought me over close, and I jumped up on the pier with my bag.

What I didn't see from the restaurant was there was an eight-foot fence in the way. That wasn't going to stop me; without hesitation, I climbed over. I started walking towards the boat and found a security station in between me and my goal. I stated my intention to the security guard, and he told me it was a secure area, "You need credentials to get in." "Where can I get them?" I asked. He pointed in a direction. I believe he was trying to get me to go away so he could call the police, but I walked away in that direction.

Large dump trucks were driving toward the freighter passing me, I stopped one or two and asked for help. One said he would help by talking to someone for me, but I didn't run into him again after that. I made it into a couple of buildings, found people in one, and they told me where I could go. When I got there, the building was empty. I wound up just stopping and taking a break for a bit on the side of the road.

After about five minutes of that, I was surrounded by five different types of police. I didn't realize it before this moment, but I was in a highly secured area. They started questioning me, and I told them what I wanted to do but lied about why. I knew they wouldn't understand, being chased by demons and such. In handcuffs, I was about to be arrested until they spoke with my family. My mother explained to the police what was going on with me, and once they started asking me about that, things turned fast.

An ambulance was called, and I was admitted into a psych ward. My three days there is a blur. I was drugged up and in a zombie-like state. I was released with more medications into my mother's care. She set me up in her spare room. I didn't mind, I didn't want to be alone anymore, and it was almost Christmas. My brother and Dad went and brought Vickie back. Still covered in mud inside and out, they cleaned her up nice for me.

I didn't want to be on the antipsychotic drugs anymore. They thought I was crazy; I knew I wasn't. I needed help; I couldn't do it alone. I reached out to someone I had met online a while back. She is an energy healer and helped me before. I knew it was her higher self that guided me back home from Texas and through some of my difficult times. I asked her for help, and she agreed that I needed to stop the meds. I started weaning myself off, and when I was off them, my clairaudience kicked back on, and all I heard were the demons. It wasn't for long, though, and I was able to keep things under control until our session.

The session was amazing, and I no longer heard my demons. The most special thing was we realized we have a very special connection and have lived many lives together. We eventually discovered we are twin flames. Everything improved from there. The day after I closed on my house, I packed up my things to drive a thousand miles to meet her. We set out across the country on the road trip of our lifetime, and as fate would have it, we landed in Utah and decided to stay.

What I learned is that discernment is very important. As men, we're taught to suppress our feelings, to act. I was so caught up in my spirituality that I wasn't taking the time to feel into my actions. Messages we receive through our gifts tell us what we need to take us and where we need to go. They aren't always accurate; they're what we need. Not every message is from a correct source either. Use discernment for everything before you act. "Question the answers," to quote the title of my favorite Mighty Mighty Bosstones album. Every once in a while, I might hear from my so-called demons, but now I know to use discernment; I recognize the right from the wrong.

Ken Shepardson is a techy, metalhead quantum healer, medium, and a channel. Still working in the 3D world as a maintenance technician, Ken's multidimensional roots have a strong Arcturian background as well as lives on Lyra, Andromeda, and Sirius. He brings this into healing sessions along with a strong connection with angels, especially Archangel Michael. Connect with him and his twin flame healer wife at: LiKeEnergyHealing.com or LiKeEnergyHealing@gmail.com

CHAPTER 9

FINDING MY CENTER
OF CALMNESS

PERSONAL POWER TO THINK,
GROW AND LEAD

DK Warinner, Founder, Center of Calmness®

Has there ever been a time in your life, or perhaps a time with someone you love, where you or they felt so much stress, overwhelm, anxiety, or depression coursing through their veins, clouding their mind, and weakening the body that they wanted nothing more than to escape that moment so that crippling feeling would go away?

The idea would be to escape for good if possible—or if not, even for just a few minutes, long enough to catch their breath, get a cool drink, or take in a ray of sunshine before jumping back into battle?

I've met so many people on my journey that live in fight or flight, one trigger away from overwhelm or potentially a total meltdown—feeling constant pressure to do more, be more, and, either accidentally or intentionally, find ways to add more stress into their lives until that time when there is a breakdown in well-being that forces a course correction, one way or the other.

Does it really have to be this way?

Is there a way to forever escape the cycle of stress and find a center of calmness?

My journey of finding my center of calmness began accidentally, at age two. I was strapped into the child seat on an old Raleigh ten-speed. Dating myself here. The child seat had thin web straps and almost no padding or protection. My dad rode his Raleigh on neighborhood streets pretty fast from a two-year-old's point of view!

On this day, that all-knowing intuition in two-year-old me was ringing. Something was off. I needed to not be there!

But this was my dad, and I was two! I had no voice to change the course.

I remember feeling that pressure of something being wrong, and potentially desperately wrong, during the ride, right up to the point where Dad lost his balance, and the bike went down, taking me with it.

I don't remember if I sustained any injuries, but my subconscious mind made sure this was not going to happen again.

From that moment on, every time little me or, later in life, big me found himself in a situation that remotely resembled this bike ride at two years old, I'd instantly fall into a doubled-over panic where I felt completely out of control! It didn't take very long for the stress from those panic attacks (hundreds of them) to build up into chronic anxiety that I carried through my school years, college, and into adult professional life. This anxiety impacted my relationships as well as my achievements. Never feeling secure in myself, I related badly with colleagues, family, and friends and achieved much as a way of validating my worth. The combination of these factors had me crashing into limiting barriers to achievement as I bumped into relationship barriers and a strong sense of self-criticism.

Even so, I pressed on, achieving three college degrees and an engineering career turned managerial. I found my way to a corporation that groomed its key managers by rotating them through corporate and facility assignments until they were ready to assume a leadership role at one of their business units. After a rocky start, I found my groove and started moving up the ladder, achieving two promotional transfers at both of the company's largest groups.

As I walked into day one of that second transfer into a new management opportunity, that same intuition of that two-year-old me rang again.

Something's wrong.

I don't want to be here!

It's not that I'd been exempt from panic or anxiety the prior few years, but with a constant drive to learn and grow, it had taken a bit of a back seat. Later, I discovered I had only suppressed the anxiety and stress, meaning I couldn't feel it as it continued to build within me.

But, on the surface, outside of the occasional need to control panic while riding in the back seat of a small rental car full of colleagues, things seemed okay.

My new boss, the Operations Director of the facility, a plant that made several thousand units of mobile equipment annually, met me at the door.

"Good morning!"

"How was your trip--when did you get in?"

I extended my hand for the usual welcoming handshake.

He turned and went back through the door without returning the handshake!

What seemed like a small gesture of rudeness or posturing led to a culture of corporate toxicity I had never experienced before.

Up until then, I worked in supportive team environments where even newcomers were supported to take on their new roles. Complaints were reserved for those already given ample opportunity to acclimate to their roles.

I walked straight into corporate hell, by comparison.

Two managers were yelling at each other within my first half day.

"Your team didn't finish the design in time!"

"You didn't work with us, and that's why we're late!"

Ongoing, useless conflict.

The stress level on the office floor was palpable throughout. One day, I printed a personal document required for a car loan, and the person who found it there, rather than extending the courtesy of bringing it to me, proceeded to distribute it through the office, creating a lot of sarcastic laughter and a short HR nightmare.

That was only the first month.

Over time, I began to realize the boss I worked for was far more adept at getting people fired than he was at developing them for success. I witnessed one colleague targeted and eventually terminated, and eventually, the rumors swirled about me as well. This might have had something to do with the reason why I was advertised to be transferred to a business unit to eventually take on the operations role when the boss retired—turf protection at its finest. If I succeeded, he might be encouraged to retire early.

One engineer pulled me aside one day to say, "He's coming for you, hard. Hold on!"

You guessed it. Full panic triggered. It wasn't hard to find evidence of the boss working on running me out of town after that.

This was no longer simple anxiety. It was overwhelm. It was hard getting out of bed and hard to make it through more than a half-day at the office without some kind of a break. Some evenings, my legs felt very, very heavy, like I was walking through mud.

I found ways to excuse my situation, even applying familiar, counterproductive coping mechanisms. Deep down, I knew they were potentially debilitating!

It was a downward spiral that appeared sure to end my career as I knew it. What mental condition would I be in after that?

At that moment, something deep within me woke up.

You've got to fix this.

Suddenly, I could clearly see what I could see all along:

It didn't have to be this way!

My moment of epiphany was confirmed when I reached the ocean one day and, wading in, found:

My tremendously high anxiety was gone!

For just a few minutes, I had no anxiety at all.

I just stood there for a moment, taking in a ray of sunshine, smelling the salt of the sea.

Now, to be clear, the battle wasn't over. As soon as I left the ocean, my anxiety quickly returned. For a while, the ocean became my place of perfect peace, where I could find a moment of freedom.

I found practical ways to address my career situation as well. I moved away and changed my career path away from corporate politics and toward specialized skills development. When I found more of the same workplace situations without much improvement, I began to lose hope of finding the perfect company.

That was the moment a new solution emerged!

What if it doesn't have to be that way?

What if I could eliminate the anxiety?

This, the same anxiety that so many depend on drugs, talk therapy, coping mechanisms, supplements, rituals, and a host of other palliatives to temporarily ease, only to return again and cause more damage as the cortisol spikes take their toll.

What if I could?

I began to reach into my past for practices that might potentially help—martial arts and meditation. I continued my research into chi flow and practices designed to leverage that body-mind phenomenon. I made more trips to the ocean to practice what I learned to be grounding.

Then, it hit me—the truth that would echo through my life, past, present, and future, and flow through me to touch many other lives:

Anxiety and stress are generated from within!

Contrary to my popular belief, there wasn't a situation or event that created stress for me. It's my response to all the happenings in life that generate a buildup of stress until that manifests as anxiety and eventually amplifies into chronic anxiety and overwhelm.

Seems simple, but many millions don't know it.

If I'm creating the stress, I can eliminate it.

I began working on a meditation specifically tuned to clear emotional stress and anxiety, leveraging common and less-common techniques in a new way. As I went forward into more consistent and regular practice, I found that red days (highly anxious dawn to dark) gave way to yellow days (highly stressed with occasional triggered anxiety). Until one day, I woke up one Sunday morning, green (without any noticeable stress or anxiety!)

I had found my place of calmness.

Once I found it, I could return. In the months that followed, I developed a simple five to ten-minute exercise that brought me from stress to clear through a sequence of progressive relaxation and visualization—the DK Method for Stress and Anxiety Elimination.

I shared the method with a realtor; she canceled her plans to pursue a drug-based solution and, achieving mastery over anxiety, became a broker. "I've just found so much peace in going to this technique that DK teaches."

I shared the method with a tax advisor; he went from often-triggered and exhausted to energetic and leaning into new adventures as host of a growing community of committed entrepreneurs. "I was able to take my energy from a state of 8 or 9 on the anxiety or stress scale—now I'm sitting at a 1 or 2!"

I shared the method with a theater producer; her creativity skyrocketed in the moments after each meditation, and she went on to create a new business serving entrepreneurs with high converting graphics. "I was just boiling over with inspiration. . .[The DK Method] opened all the passageways in my mind!"

These three and other clients have all found a new reality regarding anxiety and stress: It doesn't have to be that way!

And there was more.

What's the benefit of having a solution, a method that's always available that produces instant calmness?

When that method is applied to that stress engine that drives most people, the constant carriage of stress is replaced by a constant, deep sense of inner peace and calmness.

That gut reaction of spiking stress before taking action is replaced by a different pro-action of producing calmness and allowing that natural energy that flows with clarity and focus to produce greater results.

That's when I found my center of calmness.

Once I began to leverage that center of calmness in my life, amazing things started to happen!

I found greater clarity in my mind and ability to <u>think</u>.

I could receive ideas and solutions quickly and easily without a cloud of confusion. This was effective in my own business as well as for my clients. As I meditated on their business objectives, I found new pathways for them and insightful questions to guide their thoughts.

I widened my perception and perspective and found new possibilities to <u>grow</u>.

I ventured forth from tried and true methods and solutions I developed for myself and others into the unknown, willing to engage client challenges in the moment and allow solutions for them to come forth in my mind by maintaining curiosity and staying "in the question."

No longer triggered by most types of conflict, I found calm energy particularly effective in <u>lead</u>ing.

Calmness became my trademark—a way of life and being that became so noticeable a transformational coach picked me out of a crowd on Zoom to note that I "Maintained a high level of calmness throughout" a challenging 34-hour weekend event.

Now, I regularly enjoy receiving unsolicited comments about my calmness—my way of being!

My Center of Calmness: Personal Power to Think, Grow and Lead.

Who can benefit from finding their Center of Calmness?

The DK Method for Stress and Anxiety Elimination works quickly and progressively without drugs or devices. It works anyplace and anytime, positioning this powerful method to support:

High achievers.

Those who see a higher standard of performance for themselves personally and professionally often add stress intentionally through aggressive development, building to deadlines, handling criticism, delegating to others who might not share their vision, and competition. Developing a center of calmness provides a way of achieving clarity and focus that works for anyone!

Leaders of all kinds.

Leaders find themselves in the personal and interpersonal conflict regularly, each event potentially becoming a trigger of stress created from within. The art of managing multiple personality types, managing expectations, leading teams, handling ever-changing social dynamics, running meetings, and driving progress typically has driven high levels of stress. Now the art of leadership can become "Calm Leadership" when leading from a center of calmness.

Those challenged with long-term anxiety and stress challenges.

"The wolf that wins is the one you feed." By mastering The DK Method of Stress and Anxiety Elimination, those who have longstanding struggles with anxiety and stress can find release when they have established a center of calmness they can return to and find that inner peace that exposes anxiety for what it is, a fear-driven illusion.

Individuals in high-stress environments.

Corporate environments, public institutions, developing situations of many kinds, and anywhere the public at large is focused can easily trigger rapidly accumulating and amplifying levels of stress and anxiety, especially when individuals find themselves without much positional power, in conflict, in political situations, and with high-pressure deadlines. Having a simple method to quickly reach a center of calmness is highly supportive to maximize clarity, focus, and power in these critical situations without accumulating toxic stress and without becoming overwhelmed.

I look forward to hearing the story of you finding your center of calmness and activating your personal power to think, grow and lead!

DK Warinner is one of those high achievers--born to a professor of Physics and Mechanical Engineering who founded Physics Departments at universities and served as a researcher in areas of gas levitation and nuclear reactor cooling, and a specialist in Asian Studies, DK followed in his parent's footsteps of striving to achieve.

DK's personal struggle with anxiety is actually coupled with a strong determination to continue his own track record of high-level achievement to become a life-changer. This struggle and determination led DK to the method he now shares with people worldwide. By assessing the stages of stress-triggered anxiety and focusing on physical, emotional, and mental steps to create the path out of that anxiety, DK immersed himself and emerged victoriously! The DK Method for Stress and Anxiety Elimination was born--a simple proven method, teachable in one session, with life-long impacts of eliminating stress and enabling a higher level of success in business and life--with no drugs or therapy.

The Center of Calmness was founded to empower individual achievers with The DK Method for Stress and Anxiety Elimination. The Center of Calmness also coaches and trains individuals in applying mindsets and skillsets that powerfully enable individuals to shift personally and professionally from debilitating "Stress Driving You" into empowering "You Driving Your Success."

DK offers group coaching, 1-on-1 support, and high-performance mentorship from the Center of Calmness – Your Personal Power to Think, Grow and Lead TM.

RelaxMeDK@gmail.com

https://www.facebook.com/centerofcalmness

CHAPTER 10

SCREAMING TO BE SEEN

FORGIVENESS OF SELF THROUGH HONESTY AND ACCEPTANCE

Kenny DesChamp, B.Mus. B.Ed.

My father threw his spent cigarette down on the gravel driveway and walked away. I watched it smoldering and smelled the hot, biting odor of the tobacco. My five-year-old mind was curious: *I wonder what that tastes like? Maybe I'll give it a try.*

When no one was in sight I picked it up, put it to my lips, and inhaled. I got really high and loved the feeling, but only for a minute. Moments later, I felt deathly ill and thought I was going to throw up. At that early moment, unbeknownst to me, I'd crossed an invisible and dangerous line. Nicotine was the gateway drug that fueled the beginning of a lifelong pattern of dishonesty, addiction, and lies.

Having been the longest baby recorded in the history of the hospital, my growth rate showed no signs of slowing. Mother often told me the story of strangers insisting that she put me down so I could learn to walk, not knowing I wasn't old enough to do so. Such comments must have been hard for her. By the time I was twelve years old, I'd grown to over six feet, was unusually thin, and frequently met with stares. I resented the negative attention.

Early body pain manifested itself on the playground. I couldn't keep up with the other children, and my mother noticed a limp.

She repeatedly insisted, "Doctor, there's something wrong with him!"

But at each visit, he dismissed her with, "Look at those rosy cheeks. They show otherwise."

True to my mother's suspicion, at age nine, a specialist diagnosed me with scoliosis. It was severe enough that I was required to wear a Milwaukee Brace for 22 hours each day for six years. It was painfully barbaric, with one steel rod extending from my lower abdomen, up the front of my chest to a padded chin rest and metal collar, and one steel rod on either side of my spine, all held together with straps and a thick leather girdle.

The stares that once followed me became more frequent and pronounced, and my resentments deepened. Mom was right; there was something wrong with me, a fact I couldn't accept. I saw my crooked reflection in the mirror and felt only disdain. I sang myself to sleep at night; it made me feel connected somehow.

On the one hand, I was relieved to know there was indeed something wrong with me, yet my feeling of differentness deepened my insecurities and feelings of inadequacy. I told lies to anyone who'd listen, acted out in class, and took things from others that didn't belong to me. I was desperate to fit in anywhere I could.

The girls in my third-grade classroom defended me against bullies, but their patronizing nods and condescending "Hi, Ken"s as they quickly looked away were delivered as if they were doing me a favor. When I got to high school, I wasn't allowed in the gym for fear of injury (and liability, I suppose), so I was instead confined to an empty room during class and made to write out the rules of the games from a textbook. I felt hurt, isolated, and angry. *Am I that repulsive?*

But I continued to draw strength from singing. It allowed me to feel seen, sometimes in unusual ways. I was a soloist at our church and was chosen to carry a great wooden crucifix at the front of the choir during the processional. I deliberately carried the cross much higher than intended, delighting in the facial expressions of the horrified parishioners as I set the top of the cross on a collision course with the ceiling light, only to drop and catch it at the last second. This weekly antic never ceased to mortify the congregation.

With funding from the Rotary Club, I was able to go to summer camp for what we were then called crippled children, a label all of us deeply resented. I felt comfortable at Camp Merrywood among those who were challenged as I was. I loved our music director; we shared the healing of singing together. Unfortunately, this is where I learned to smoke cigarettes in earnest.

By this time, the ingrained and ever-increasing resentments and my need to fit in resulted in two activities: singing and chain-smoking cigarettes. In some way, both were places for me to feel comforted. One was a place for me to heal, and the other formed an escape route to drugs and alcohol. By the time I was 16, I was drinking heavily and dropping acid.

In spite of my substance abuse, I practiced singing day and night, so I could develop my skills and be seen as worthy, even though I couldn't run or toss a ball. What I didn't see clearly was my need for solace in my own voice.

I fit into the local music scene, belting out tunes in one band or another. I basked in the limelight and reveled in the applause, the slaps on the back, and the complimentary comments. I feigned great confidence, yet beneath the façade, I couldn't accept the way I was, even after the brace was gone.

I attended high school during the day and played a house gig at a local bar six nights a week. I backed up strippers, smoked, drank heavily with the older musicians, and thought I was grown up.

When my father died of emphysema as a result of his nicotine addiction, I blamed myself.

He often warned, "Don't come near me with a cold. I could end up in the hospital with pneumonia and die."

I'd come home from a gig the weekend before with a cold, and within a few days, he was rushed to the hospital and died. He wasn't even buried before I broke into his locked, black medicine box beside his bed, stole his many cartons of cigarettes, and chain-smoked them all. I vowed to die as he had; I believed I'd killed him. The depression and feelings of guilt that followed lingered for decades.

Needless to say, things at school didn't go well. My grades took a nosedive, and the duality of my personality showed its two faces once again. On the one hand, I cared very little about anything and needed no one, but on the other, I was desperate to be seen. I wore platform shoes that added three inches to my six-foot-six-inch height. Make-up, nail polish, and black lipstick were my norm. A halter-top was my piece de la resistance that I wore with heavily patched jeans. Long, permed hair framed my sullen face. I shoplifted and stole from strangers and acquaintances for the thrill. The dichotomy of what I wanted and needed was a bizarre paradox.

Eventually, I dropped out of school and toured Canada with a rock band. As exciting as it may seem, the long drives in a van, unsavory hotels where we spent our nights, and evenings where we played, sang, smoked, drank, and artfully mistreated the women who came to our beds, were anything but exciting or glamorous.

It didn't take long before I was out of control and couldn't manage my life. More often than not, I owed more money to the bar than I made. I hated myself. One night, in the middle of a set, I was so depressed that I spat at my reflection in a mirror that adorned the back wall of the stage. It was a wonder we weren't tossed into the street. I was so arrogant and full of self-loathing that I wouldn't have cared.

Not long after that incident, I hit my first bottom. My dream of forging a career in music was dashed out of fear of failing at something I loved, which I seemingly did regardless. But from that bottom came one of the most fortuitous but unlikely decisions of my life. I quit the band and applied to university. It sounds like a wise choice, but the truth is, I had no other place to turn. I'd hated school! Nevertheless, I was accepted as a mature student and managed to scrape through my first year despite my heavy drinking.

The second bottom came in my third year. I'd been drinking alone in my dorm non-stop for three weeks. Empty beer and liquor bottles were piled high in a corner. I couldn't keep food down and was shaking uncontrollably. My liver felt like it was going to flip out of my body. The pain in my abdomen was unbearable.

I called Alcoholics Anonymous in the middle of the night in a serious crisis because I was suicidal. Four men were in my room within minutes. Somehow they convinced me to pour my alcohol down the sink. They watched over me all night. With their help, I managed to detoxify and get sober for the first time in years. They took me to two meetings a day. After a week or so, the shakes and liver pain subsided.

During those five years, I got married, achieved some creative success, and stayed sober most of the time. When my wife would leave town for a conference, I'd drink until the day she got home and then lie about it.

In 1985 I attained an honors music degree with concentrations in voice and composition. The local music scene was vibrant at the time, and I considered staying in the city to pursue a career in music, but I didn't trust myself. So I took a day job I never wanted and kept it for 30 years. I thought it would be safe and keep me from drinking, but I was wrong.

Lies, dishonesty, and addiction caught up with me again after 29 years of marriage. I lost everything except my job. My daughter wouldn't talk to me, and her loss was unbearable. It was the darkest time in my life. I moved into a tiny one-bedroom apartment in the former post office building where my father had worked for over 20 years. I was sure he'd be ashamed of me. Yet looking back at what happened next, I'm sure he was watching over me.

Karin and I met in the underground parking garage of the apartment building, where our vehicles faced each other. Our introductions went something like this:

"Hi, I'm Ken. I had to leave my wife."

"I'm Karin. I had to leave my husband."

"Separation agreements suck."

"Yeah, I know."

I liked her immediately and could tell the feelings were mutual. Besides being a teacher, Karin was a yoga enthusiast, world traveler, and lay worship leader. *I wonder what Dad would think of her?* When she invited me to her apartment for coffee one day, and I looked out her living room window into the courtyard, I was dumbfounded.

Dad had been the postmaster in this building, and Karin's apartment was where his catwalk was located. From her sparkling white kitchen through her brightly colored living room, he'd spent every working day. I envisioned my fiery, redheaded, freckled father and heard him voice his approval of this woman I was yet to know as Mrs. DesChamp.

Meanwhile, the sambuca and vodka flowed. I was in several bands; in addition to my day job, I played in local bars on weekends. Soon alcohol wasn't enough to dull my pain. Additionally, I opted for pills and then began at age 54 (yes, it's true) using cocaine. Coke gripped me immediately, and I couldn't stop. I didn't eat or sleep, and my 195-pound body quickly shrunk to 139 pounds. I was a mere skeleton. Friends were worried I'd die and told me so. I didn't care. *If you don't like what you see, don't look.* When I reflect on that time, I was probably only months from death.

I had a wake-up call one night after a gig. I was packing up my guitar when I looked up at a face I hadn't seen before. A shoddily dressed young man with long, dirty black hair stood before me. He reminded me of a disheveled David Suzuki. His lips started moving.

"Who dug you up?"

"What the hell?"

"You're as white as a sheet!"

"I don't like the sun." I added awkwardly, "You get it, right?"

The man, whose skin was decidedly dark, made a strange, rather frightening face, took his glasses off, glared at me, and bore his teeth. His eyes were crazy!

"Do I look like the sun bothers me?" he scowled.

I was taken aback and a bit frightened, so I tried to change the subject.

"Are you a musician?"

"I used to be a drummer."

"Do you still play?"

"No. I didn't want to look like you!"

I closed my guitar case and looked up, but he'd gone—disappeared. I was used to this venue, watched patrons come and go, and recognized the regulars. But this strange fellow seemed to suddenly appear and just as suddenly vanish! How could a perfect stranger who'd never seen me before recognize how sick I was?

Not long after talking with whom I now affectionately call The Angel of Death, I sank to a new low. The bottoms I'd repeatedly hit were gone. This time there wasn't a bottom.

With the help of a mental health agency, I started seeing a psychiatrist via an online telehealth network. He was compassionate but forthright.

"If you don't show up for your next appointment, I won't be surprised."

"Why?"

He leaned in close to the camera and looked directly at me. His face and eyes filled the screen. "You'll likely be dead."

His words shook me to the core. No doctor had ever said this to me. That very day, February 18th, 2014, I stopped drinking and using completely. It was excruciatingly difficult, but I wanted to live and longed for my daughter to be back in my life. The withdrawal lasted weeks and was horrific.

The following week, after 30 years, I retired from my day job. Karin took me to dinner to celebrate. I felt sick from withdrawal but tried not to let on. At one point, I expressed sorrow and remorse for losing my daughter. She listened but didn't judge. She said she could see a light that shone deep inside and told me, "Everything you want to be, you already are."

Karin's words rendered me speechless, and I broke down. She'd seen in me something that I and everyone else had been blind to. Weeks later, when she told me she loved me, my only thought was, *Why?* I told her about my addictions, and she didn't flinch. She didn't tell me to quit drinking, smoking, or using; she had only one condition: "Never lie to me."

What a demand! *How, after a lifetime of lying, am I supposed to do that?* I persisted in my attempts to be honest with her and others, which allowed me to get honest with myself. It took years, and I shed a lot of tears. I still struggle, but I try to remember that if I practice honesty and self-acceptance, I can forgive myself.

Slowly but surely, I learned humility, my confidence grew, and I became able to manage my emotions. My self-esteem improved. Eventually, my daughter came back to me. How grateful I am for that!

My nicotine addiction was still alive and well, but through harm reduction in the form of nicotine reduction therapy and counseling, I was finally able to lay it to rest. My nicotine abstinence date is exactly a year after my sobriety date.

Four years passed. My relationship with Karin was solid, and we decided to get married. Our private, intimate wedding was beautiful. We purchased a small home with an extra bedroom in which I planned to build a recording studio. At last, I could do what I loved: compose and sing my music. But there remained one problem.

The room remained untouched. I couldn't bear to stand inside, unbox my equipment, or set it up. I'd never been creative without being drunk or stoned. Anxiety and depression set in. After several months I forced myself to go in and work. I lasted five minutes. The next day I lasted ten. The next day, 15. Over time I managed to put everything together and plug it in. Finally, I stood and stared at the microphone before me. I bit my lip and felt fear grip me. My heart pounded. With great trepidation, I placed the headphones over my ears.

"Check, one, two. . ."

Then it happened. My eyes closed. I placed a palm on my abdomen and touched my throat gently with the other. I took a tentative breath. My mouth opened, and I sang a long vowel. It was a plaintive yet peaceful melody that seemed to come out of nowhere. *I hear my voice. I'm at peace.*

Today I spend as much time as possible creating and producing original music. Most of my compositions are influenced by lived experience with addiction and my gratitude for freedom from its powerful grip. Presently I have enough mastered material to release a new work every three months for the next year and a half. I'm grateful that I can finally express myself through my voice.

There are still days when I regret my past but the work of acceptance, the quest to be honest, support for and active involvement with a fellowship of people who share their experience, strength, and hope with each other, and the practice of living in the present, are keys to my contented sobriety. They allow me to forgive myself and, in turn, continue to use my voice to relate to others who might have traveled a similar path. I found my voice and saved my life.

 **Kenny DesChamp** has been in the music industry for 48 years as an independent recording artist, performer, composer, and teacher. He is a graduate of Queen's University in Kingston, Ontario, Canada, where he majored in voice and composition. His interest in twelve-tone, whole-tone, and other alternative scale structures, as well as aleatoric approaches to composition, are obvious influences. DesChamp's music is strongly influenced by lived experience with addiction and recovery. Check out Kenny DesChamp on all music streaming platforms.

Currently, Kenny works with the Peterborough Drug Strategy, where he sits on a municipal advisory panel to help make recommendations to various organizations and agencies dedicated to serving those who continue to suffer from addiction.

As a volunteer driver for the local Children's Aid Society, Ken gleans great satisfaction in giving back to the community. He is abundantly grateful.

Website: https://kennydeschamp.com/home

Facebook: https://www.facebook.com/kennydeschampmusician

Instagram: https://www.instagram.com/kennydeschamp/

YouTube:

https://www.youtube.com/channel/UC53Ixq-a8od0JScrCVQO2HA

Spotify: https://open.spotify.com/artist/3a8AghyJZvIv86NnhdASWj

CHAPTER 11

CALLED TO ACCEPTANCE

THE GIFT OF SHATTERED BELIEFS

Matt Segebartt

I sat in the back row of the conference center and heard the speaker say the words, "I only trust people with scars." As I turned the phrase over and over in my mind, it resonated with me. It beautifully connected with the story of a man named Jesus who had scars. This was familiar rhetoric that somehow allowed me to connect some critical dots.

As I navigate life, the concept of this phrase has become a guide to me. The first half of my life was characterized by a belief that hiding certain parts of myself was required for acceptance, for God's acceptance. Every aspect of my existence and daily routine was connected in some way to the church or the morality that the teachings of the church outlined. Jesus was involved in every aspect of my daily life. I was told he cared about what I ate, how I treated my body, what I listened to, my thoughts, my relationships, and of course, the music I enjoyed. It was understood that he not only cared, but if I were to eat or listen to something that was considered not good, my membership card for heaven was in jeopardy. It was emphasized that hell was a real place, and those who did not make it to heaven only had hell as an alternative destination. If my thoughts were not in alignment with the teachings of the church, then, of course, it was my thoughts that needed to change. If Whitney Houston was discovered in my CD player, there were serious conversations about the direction of my life and the eternal consequences of my choices.

As a sensitive child, I was very in tune and aware of what it felt like to please or displease others. This desire to please became the poison that led to significant woundedness. The healing of those wounds and recognizing the remaining scars is what my story and the second half of my life are all about.

Depression stalked me like a black cloud. I was living what many would call a good life. I was married with three healthy kids, had a religion degree, was ordained, and was pastoring my grandparents' and parents' denominational church. I was a third-generation Christian and knew all the right answers to most of life's difficult questions. I preached sermons with the right blend of humility and conviction and was proud that I contributed a peaceful presence to my congregation. When my beliefs began to have cracks and my wife of 17 years told me she felt a significant distance in our relationship; my soul retreated into depression. The two hardest things for me to look at were divorce and questioning if my church was wrong in its teachings on this subject. My emotional health began to suffer. I went to my doctor in search of medication to help ease the ache. He gave the standard survey to decide if I qualified for depression medication. I checked the boxes for relational stress, financial stress, a recent move, recent death in the family, and several others. When he looked at my responses, I felt justified in my hurt when he said, "I'll prescribe you those meds immediately."

One of the Ten Commandments states, "Thou shalt not lie." My depression was gaining a foothold because I was facing the very real dilemma of either becoming honest with myself and others or keeping things hidden and continuing to live the life I was currently living. By extension, this felt like a lie, but I also had to give myself the grace to acknowledge that I had not been intentionally deceptive. My mental health was compromised by living in this dilemma. I pondered if I should talk about the truth and potentially lose my marriage, community, ordination, friends, and family. Or should I keep living as I had been, knowing it was not authentic?

I do not like conflict, and this was almost more than I could take. I'd wake up every night and repeat to myself, *don't think, don't think, don't think*. That, of course, did not work. I was not sleeping; I knew where my church stood on the specific issue I was pondering. I also knew I could not keep doing what I was doing.

As a way to cope, I started reading, researching, listening to podcasts, talking to trusted friends, and reaching out to strangers for understanding. I found a book, *Torn* by Justin Lee, that addressed some of the same thoughts and issues I was dealing with. To my utter surprise, the book gave me the first inklings of what felt like hope. I was on a depressive downward spiral and the thoughtful logic presented in this book allowed some of the desperation to seep out of my poisoned soul. It was confusing to interact with both hopefulness and sadness. Hopefulness because for the first time, I could sense a graciousness in a belief structure that allowed me to be different. Sadness because I knew if I adopted this new approach, my family, friends, and known religious community would likely dismiss me. I would become a storyline where the people I knew would shake their heads and say, "How sad. Matt is now deceived and has embraced sinfulness."

To be clear, what was changing was my belief structure. For most of my life, I was absolutely sure I was not gay because I did not want to dress up in women's clothes. I'm embarrassed to admit that my construct about the gay lifestyle consisted of two things: men who were promiscuous and men who dressed up in drag. I did not want either of these things, so, therefore, I could not be gay. I was beginning to understand the gay experience is the same as the heterosexual experience, complicated and unique. With these things in mind, I decided to attend a conference. I was willing to go because it was connected with Justin Lee. I had found healing in the book, and because of that, thought I could possibly find additional healing at the conference.

I sat in my hotel room staring out the window at the Denver Convention Center directly across the street. My trip from the Pacific Northwest to attend this conference in Colorado was a secret. I have family in the mile-high city, but I did not want them to know I was there. I was very uncomfortable being there myself, and aside from a few trusted friends, I really did not want anyone to know. I sat in my room, unmoving, for several hours. Walking through the doors to the seminar felt like it would be a monumental step of self-disclosure, and my stomach churned.

This conference took place in January 2018 when I was 43 years old. The church where I grew up and worked was the only community I had ever known. My entire education, from elementary to college, as well as my professional life, was all connected to this church. My very presence at this Christian LGBTQIA affirming conference felt like a version of heresy.

Fear and sadness struck me for the thousandth time on the plane ride to Denver. Tears flowed down my face as I considered the reality of my life. There were so many unanswered questions, so many fears of the unknown. I thought about my kids. I never wanted to hurt anyone, and somehow just acknowledging what was true for me felt like a betrayal to my family and community. I considered unhealthy family patterns and my powerful desire to please people. I contemplated scriptures about being "fearfully and wonderfully made" and how "man looks at the outside, but God looks at the heart." The dilemma between voicing what was true for me and losing everything that mattered felt unfair and terrifying. It was also confusing, *I'm the same guy, nothing is different,* I told myself. For over a year, I tried to understand and accept that I was gay. I was never given language to understand my attraction. I quietly listened to nature versus nurture conversations through the years and heard phrases like, "Love the sinner, not the sin." I inaccurately received the message that being gay was all about sex, a choice made by people who were not able to control their lusts. This did not feel like it applied to what I was experiencing, and yet I did not have other information to make sense of what I had always felt.

I finally mustered the courage to walk in the doors of the convention center. The person behind the registration counter kindly greeted me and asked, "Would you like a blue or a red lanyard?" I asked, "Why does the color of my name tag matter?" He explained, "If you opt for a red one, nobody will take your picture at the event." I immediately put the red lanyard on, took my program, and found a back-row seat to recover. I was grateful they understood that some people wanted to remain anonymous. I just wished I could be invisible.

The time of worship had begun, and I sat there in the tension of enjoying meaningful singing of familiar hymns in a very unfamiliar setting. Anxiety was welling up in me, and when a person I perceived to be a man wearing a dress sat down beside me, every fiber of my being wanted to scream, *these are not my people, what am I doing here?* I looked at the program and discovered the keynote speaker for the night was a transgender man who identified as gay. *How the hell did I get here, and what vortex of evil was I participating in?*

I took a deep breath and told myself that it was normal to feel uncomfortable. I also knew what I was feeling was discomfort, not the conviction to leave. If anything, I felt a divine call to stay in my place and let the experience play out. If the guy in a dress next to me was accepted, then maybe I would be accepted too.

I sat there and thought, sang, and listened. In that space, I had what I refer to as my third conversion. The first one was when I was baptized at the age of 12. The second was when I was in college and felt like I understood grace and love for the first time.

The speaker told his story of knowing from an early age that he did not feel like he belonged in his own body. He told about hiding and shame. He told about cutting his flesh as a way to numb and release the pain and confusion. He candidly spoke about his mental health and the judgmental statements he heard about how "those people" are just confused and messed up. He gave scientific examples of physiological and anatomical anomalies that are relatively common in humans. He spoke about being made in the image of God, which is so much more than anatomy. He spoke about fashion as a cultural construct and differing masculine and feminine roles with examples from other cultures. He spoke about the original Biblical languages and showed that scripture could be interpreted in integrity to be inclusive. He explained that the word "homosexual" was not even translated as such until 1946. He made the point that we love the diversity of nature, but we do not appreciate the diversity of humans. He spoke about suicide rates in the LGBTQIA community, and as he talked about conformity and people-pleasing, I found myself transfixed. I had been reading and studying many of these topics and had big questions. I had been struggling to make sense of the complexity I felt. As he shared his story, I felt seen in a new and important way.

I realized I was not looking for someone to merely tell me I was okay. I loathed the idea of reinterpreting scripture to fit my needs. I was, ironically, looking for evidence of flimsy theology at this conference. If I found that, then I wouldn't need to interact with the more painful truth that what I was taught and what I had taught others was actively harming people, including myself. What I found as he spoke and as I thought of all the things I read, listened to, and personally experienced was a much more congruent, accurate, and inclusive view. It was not a world where we all understood each other or dressed to please others, but a world where uniqueness could actually be celebrated as a component of a Creator who clearly loves diversity.

As the speaker continued, he told of being discovered at the age of 18 by his dad. Up to that point, he had cut his body but had always worn concealing clothing, such as a long sleeve shirt. One night he fell asleep before covering his arms, and his dad saw his scars and cuts. His dad knelt beside the bed, woke him up, and said, "I don't know what you need, but I'm here with you no matter what." From that point on, they learned and walked together through the complicated process of transitioning.

The flood of my emotions broke, and the pain from years of hiding and being confused began to unravel. I have known I was different from the time I was seven, but I did not have words to explain why. His story was my story. I did not have open wounds, but I very much had scars on my soul. In his story, I was given the gift of a shattered faith construct and felt what acceptance could look like. He concluded by saying, "I only trust people with scars."

I deeply agree. In showing the places where we've been hurt and then healed, we participate in making the world a better place. I did not pursue this path, but I feel like it is a meaningful one. I do not regret the beautiful lessons and people with whom I've shared the road so far. I know there has been intense pain. I know there are scars, which means there has been healing. Acceptance is a hard-fought battle. I have become an ally for kindness, diversity, and complexity, and I believe every human on this planet is worthy of love, even me.

Matt Segebartt's life work is about acceptance. He enjoys being able to work with people at the intersection of religion and spirituality. Though he grew up a Christian, Matt also embraces other viewpoints and belief structures—which he describes as dual religious citizenship. He appreciates the complexity of the human experience and enjoys walking with people on the path of their unique stories. A certified spiritual director with a religion degree, he worked in organized religion for 14 years before transitioning to advocacy work to help disrupt social isolation. He teaches on the Enneagram and enjoys meeting one-to-one or with groups, virtually or in-person, and is available to speak or lead retreats. Matt lives in the Pacific Northwest and has three children, wonderful friends, a meaningful community, and a cat. He enjoys plants, boating, art, nature, and music.

To learn more, visit: www.mattsegebartt.com

CHAPTER 12

YOU *CAN* HEAL

A CLEAR PATH TO DITCHING THE WEIGHT OF OBLIGATION

Rev. Tomás Garza

"You're in the hospital," they kept telling me. "You were in a terrible car accident. Do you remember?"

"No."

"Yes, you were in a car accident, and your hip bones are shattered. We're getting you stabilized for a couple of days until you're ready to be transported for surgery."

I had no response to that. That explained the ugly white gown, orange walls, and the tubes floating all around, different varieties and thicknesses of tubes, all of which had to be attached to a needle stuck someplace inside me.

Also, it explained the pain. There was nothing else. When I drew breath, my lungs ached. When my heart beat, it sent out bursts of agony. It hurt to move. It hurt to think about moving. It hurt to think, period. I couldn't be bothered with the needles, the crushed bones, the surgery schedule—all I could think about was the pain, how badly I hurt and how long it was going to last. Probably forever.

Waking up in the hospital was hell, but the hell didn't end there. I had regained consciousness in the Intensive Care Unit in Corvallis, Oregon, and needed to be transported 90 minutes away to a large hospital in Portland.

There I would have the major surgery. I can barely remember the Corvallis ICU, and I have only one recollection of the transport, that of a lone spruce tree whizzing by against a gray bank of clouds. The next time I found myself aware of my surroundings, a full three days after the accident, I languished in pre-op. In case you're wondering, the pain hadn't gone anywhere.

The surgery, I'm told, took six hours, and I needed eight units of blood. They told me everything went well, but I don't remember much more than that. The pain still hadn't lessened, and my entire body was swollen with fluid. My hands looked twice their normal size. At one point, I had the misfortune to glance down at my testicles. Enlarged, purple, and bruised, they resembled a pair of eggplants.

I spent a total of 13 days in the hospital. The surgeons repaired my acetabulum, the bone structure surrounding the hip joint. Miraculously, the joint itself was unharmed, and I suffered no nerve or spinal cord damage. As I lay immobile and stupefied on opioid pain meds, some conversations I remember, but mostly I don't. I do recall the delicious bacon cheeseburgers from the hospital cafeteria, the barbecue chicken pizza my then-girlfriend Cindy brought me, the Thai curry, and the Burger King vanilla milkshake from my friend Norm. I also remember the three days of an IV morphine drip, the detox that followed, the night sweats, and more pain, always more pain. Toward the end, I had to learn to get around on crutches. All I wanted to do was go back to bed and eat another bacon cheeseburger. They told me my body was working so hard to heal that I could eat as many calories as I pleased, but this didn't comfort me; what I really wanted was to stand up and walk out of there. It's amazing the things we take for granted in life, like walking.

December 3, 2013, was a Tuesday, another day of child custody mediation. The night before, I remember telling Cindy, "God, tomorrow's gonna suck. I am not looking forward to this."

"How many appointments do you have?"

"Five, and they're all typical. All of them shouting at each other, all of them using their kids as weapons. You know, Tuesday. Oh, and the hour commute, too."

I practiced family and child custody mediation for nearly 13 years. When you can honestly tell people at the end of your service that you never want to see them again, you know you're in a twisted business. Every battle made me ill, but the steady stream of income and referrals meant I hadn't found the tenacity yet to leave. My resignation letters sat patiently typed and ready to go on my desk. They sat there for months.

So why hadn't I sent them? Obligation. Why had I persisted in a deeply stressful career I no longer enjoyed? Obligation. What caused me to get up the morning of December 3, shower, get dressed, have breakfast, and hop in the car to go deal with people's hostility? Again, obligation. Obligation made me do it. Obligation made me keep accepting new clients. Obligation made me sit in yet another couple's frothing stew of hatred. Obligation made me drive the car that day. Obligation—sheer duty and obligation. Because of it, I couldn't walk. Obligation landed me in the hospital. Obligation caused me—so I'm told—to pull out in front of some man's Subaru and get t-boned at 60 miles per hour. Obligation nearly killed me on the scene.

Many people suffer under the weight of obligation. I am not alone; there is nothing special about me. Each and every one of us receives indoctrination growing up. Most people call it our youth. When we think about it, though, it's a carefully constructed program of conditioning, from our parents to our siblings to society itself, our schoolteachers, friends, television and other advertising, everything. We couldn't escape it growing up if we tried. I certainly didn't.

My family hit me hard. "Intelligent young men," I was repeatedly told, "grow up to be doctors, lawyers, or politicians." Only that would do. It wasn't about happiness, after all. While they never came out and said it, the message was all about social status and prestige, of looking good despite how you may feel. At family gatherings, my grandfather used to shake my hand in greeting, slip me a 20-dollar bill, and say, "I want you to go to Harvard." For the record, I didn't, but I did wind up in law school, then child custody mediation. That's also how I wound up driving that December morning to a gig I despised, just like I had managed to do countless times before. It wasn't about happiness. Who has that luxury?

Following the accident, I found myself with nothing but time, unless, of course, you throw in pain. Still on heavy-duty meds as Christmas approached, I could not serve any mediation clients. I learned one day in an email that I had no more clients: the court system, with whom I had the referral contract, had transferred all my active cases to another mediator.

I had the pain and the medication, which I loathed because it constipated me.

What the fuck am I gonna do now? How am I supposed to make any money? God, my leg hurts. My brain does, too. What the actual fuck? I'm hungry again, but I can't move. Damn it, this sucks. God, I'm tired.

My mind went on and on like this between bouts of pain and fruitless trips to the bathroom. The days dragged along. On Christmas Eve, as we hosted a party with family and friends, I ate dinner and observed the festivities from my perch in the living room, where my adjustable hospital-style bed sat. I couldn't travel up the stairs to the bedroom, so I spent several weeks eating, sleeping, watching television, attempting to pee, and bemoaning my fate downstairs in the hospital-style bed, knowing that a long and grueling journey awaited me. I knew that pain medication wouldn't help with this one. Healing would involve a whole lot more than just prescription pills.

As I gradually learned to get around, at first on crutches, then with a cane, I had plenty of time to think. I would alternate between feeling sorry for myself and expressing genuine gratitude for simply being alive. Physical movement was a moment-to-moment struggle; each trip to the bathroom or the refrigerator took on a brand-new meaning. Routine activities suddenly required planning: *Okay, now I'm going to shift my right hip and step forward with my right foot. Then I'm going to reach out with my right hand and stabilize myself on the counter. Then I'm going to step forward with my left foot. Then I'm going to grab the refrigerator handle with my left hand and pull it open while I stabilize myself against the counter with my right hand.*

Each day looked like this. Gone were the automatic, fluid movements.

During these days of rehabilitation, my mood sank. I knew a lot of work lay ahead of me because while my body would heal itself in time, an opportunity for real healing was staring me right in the face, and I wanted to run. I wanted to hide, to turtle up in a ball on the closet floor, close my eyes, and will the work to be done already—all of it. I would dream of swimming in a warm ocean, of tropical beaches and strong cocktails, of palm trees and warmth, of sunlight. Holed up in my living room in a typical western Oregon winter, I had none of those things, and I didn't want to admit that I'd brought this whole fiasco on myself, not just the auto accident but the entire comprehensive experience.

How can this be? At some point, there's no escaping it: I was the one who applied to law school. I was the one who moved to western Oregon, and its slow, steady drizzle that falls from October to May. I was the one who began a private practice as a child custody mediator. We can blame other people or circumstances all we want, but sooner or later, we're all faced with the realization that we and only we have brought hell and convalescence on ourselves. If we are to really heal, we have to start with this honesty, with accepting full responsibility.

I didn't want to. Nobody wants to, even in the best of circumstances. Mine was awful: I hobbled around on crutches, sinking quickly into mental and emotional blackness. I faced the prospect of learning to walk again, then physical therapy, then dealing with the fact that while I finally mailed those letters and left child custody mediation behind, I had no other income. All the while, the drizzling rain kept falling. My body was healing, but not my mind. Real depression followed.

With depression, some days are brighter than others, but they're all horrible. One, in particular, stands out. In June of 2014, after I had learned to walk again, Cindy and I took an afternoon stroll. The sky was cloudy, but in western Oregon, people can't wait for clear weather; they have to carry on despite the darkness.

We started walking. I don't remember what Cindy was telling me; I do remember that I couldn't respond. I heard only sounds with no meaning. My gaze shot downward. The sky oppressed me. The air oppressed me. The ground tried to pull me in. Rather than seeing grass and evergreen trees, I saw blackness. The fringe of all objects was black, as though they possessed an evil aura. I trudged through a field of blackness, one dark step—shuffle—after another. I felt my body would crumple like an accordion. Each step took a decade.

I had no prospects. I didn't know what to do or what I wanted to do. The money was disappearing. I had done what other people expected of me, what I was supposed to do, and look now. There was no way I would ever crawl out of this blackness; its evil leached the vitality from my bones.

We got home that day, and I did curl into a ball. There on our bedroom floor, I folded like a crumpled piece of paper, and I wept. I do not know how long I stayed there. I had no idea what to do.

But I did know what to do; I just didn't want to do it—*no way in hell.*

Indoctrination is always brutal. Its weight stifles us and keeps us paralyzed, confused, enraged, and in fear. Finally, acknowledging my depression, and recognizing that I had probably been that way for years, did not help me to ask for assistance. Think about it; I was supposed to have all the answers. I was a rugged individualist, a self-sustaining survival unit. I could figure all this out. In fact, I had to. Nobody asks for help. No one. No way in hell do you ever admit you need it, and no way in hell do you ever admit you don't have all the answers. Of course, you have them!

Don't you?

I finally had to accept that the answer was no. I had no solutions. The only thing left to do was what I hadn't done. I had to ask for help in order to heal. It wouldn't be possible otherwise.

The call to the doctor's office that day was the hardest I had ever made. It far exceeded the dread I used to feel when calling a girl to ask for a date in high school. This was admitting weakness; the high school stuff was just uncertainty.

"My name is Tomás Garza," I began. "I need to schedule an appointment."

"And what's the purpose of your appointment, Tomás?"

Deep breath. Pause. "I. . .I, um, I'm depressed, and I need to talk to someone about getting on antidepressants." Just a few days later, I had them.

About three weeks later, the medication began to take effect. When I recognized that I felt lighter, Cindy and I were in Anaheim, California, for her national business convention. Sitting in a sunlit courtyard, I realized I had energy again. I no longer saw black; instead, I saw colors—the blue of the sky, the bright yellow of blooming sunflowers. Years dropped off me; wrinkles disappeared as though they had never existed. I could not remember the last time I had felt light and truly happy.

These new feelings of lightness did not eliminate the money question. After the convention, at my sister's house in Long Beach, I sat with her in the backyard, watching her dogs dig up the lawn, roll in the fresh earth, then defecate—and roll in that, too. We talked about my clean slate in life, what it's like to be on antidepressants, and the spectacle of her giant tortoises, who liked to stroll around the yard and eat what the dogs left behind.

At one point, she asked, "So you really have no idea what you're going to do?"

"Nope."

"And you're okay with that?"

"Yeah." I really was. It didn't matter that she or anyone else was incredulous; I didn't have the answers, and that was okay. I forced myself to let go of control of the outcome. I also stepped back and began to trust. The weight of obligation disappeared. Once so real and so cumbersome, it simply vanished.

To heal is to leave this weight behind. We do it by accepting healing for ourselves. Weighed down by our indoctrination and sense of duty, we struggle to do this. We believe we have all the answers. When we admit we don't have any answers, that is a healing moment. When we ask for help, that is a healing moment, too.

The path to healing is simple, disarmingly so. That's the point: once we drop our defenses and our need to control, we set our hardships to the side. Doing so is simpler than we think, and anyone can do it. Anyone can ask for help. Anyone can give up the effort to control and say, "You know what? I don't know what to do here. I don't have any of the answers, but I trust it will all work out as it's supposed to. There is nothing else I need to do right now."

And in doing nothing, we accomplish everything. We heal. We let go of the past. We ditch the weight of obligation. Then, we live.

For an exclusive video describing healing and this chapter in greater detail, visit

https://youtu.be/ai6zulnyEvA

Rev. Tomás Garza is an ordained Minister of Metaphysical Sciences and a spiritual coach and teacher. He is also a SolePath Mentor, helping people live from a place of their strengths and navigate away from their darkness toward their joy and light. He is the host of the podcast *Decide to Transform* and a long-standing video series on *A Course in Miracles*. He is a three-time published author and a Meditation Instructor, having begun a lifelong practice as a sophomore in high school, where his old hippie Geometry teacher had everyone meditate at the beginning of class each day.

Rev. Tomás' mission is to heal the illusion of separation. He enjoys guiding people on their journey of questioning the foundations of everything they have ever believed and discovering their innate healing capabilities. Should we so choose, each of us can awaken our power to heal.

Rev. Tomás lives in Surprise, Arizona, with his wife Cindy and loves the heat, hiking, and the expanse of the desert sky.

For a deeper dive into healing, listen to Tomás' podcast episode from *Decide to Transform*:

https://decidetotransform.podbean.com/e/healing

CHAPTER 13

THE SACRED CARPET

ON-RAMP TO A PATH OF TRANSCENDENCE

David D McLeod, DD, PhD, Certified Master Life Coach

Transcendent Man? Me? The phrase doesn't resonate for me, but I concede I've had an interesting, challenging, and illuminating life, and I recognize I am now well-established on a path toward *transcendence.*

Let me share with you how I found my path.

AN UNEXPECTED TRAP

I know you better than you know yourself.

When I reflect on my childhood, these words always pop into my awareness. I first heard them at the ripe old age of three! I was barely at the cognitive level of literal interpretation, so I had no conscious idea about possible underlying implications; therefore, I thought little about them. But today, I recognize the impact those eight words had on the subsequent 40 years of my life.

As a child with an independent streak bordering on rebelliousness, I was doing something that stretched Mom's patience past her limit.

"Oh, my shattered nerves!" she shrieked, her arms apparently trying to grab something invisible out of the air above her head. "Stop! Just stop!"

Mom was a decent, loving woman and not prone to violence, even when she was angry. But something in her voice triggered a warning within me, and I knew better than to continue my forbidden activity.

Red-faced, rigid, arms no longer flailing but crossed over her chest— her intense glare burned through me.

"I'm your mother," she hissed. "You are supposed to listen to me. You are supposed to do what you are told. Do you understand me?"

Frozen, quiet, fidgety, I was nodding obediently, trying to keep my bearings. There was something about Mom I hadn't seen before. Fear leaked into my heart.

Her hand swept around and snagged my wrist. "Come with me, young man!" I scrambled to keep up as she dragged me toward my bedroom.

The next thing I knew, I was on top of the changing table, Mom's hands clamped tight on both my arms. Squirming was out of the question.

"Sorry, Mommy," I squeaked. Tears spilled onto my cheek.

She leaned, squinting, close to my face. "Never mind the fake apologies! It's about time you figured this out!"

What followed was a veritable onslaught of logical reasons that she was in charge and I was supposed to obey her. Wide-eyed and breathless, I bobble-headed in mute acquiescence.

Lecture complete, she stood up again. Lip slightly upturned, finger leveled at my chest, she unleashed her secret weapon.

I know you better than you know yourself." No malice. No anger. No fanfare of any kind. Just eight simple, innocuous words, delivered in a whisper of palpable conviction.

I have no recollection how I reacted when the words landed. They came from my mother, someone I trusted, who knew me best, who took care of all my needs, who loved me, and who would never tell a lie. As a three-year-old, what reason would I have for accepting it as anything other than *absolute truth?*

In my adult mind of today, I imagine the sentence bounced around my immature head for a while. But having already accepted it as true, I probably reasoned in the typical way of three-year-olds: *If Mommy knows me better than I know myself, then Daddy must also know me better than I know myself. And if Mommy and Daddy know me better than I know myself, then Grandma and Grandpa do too.*

Pretty soon, I convinced myself that all my relatives and friends knew me better than I knew myself. And that list rapidly expanded to include teachers, church ministers, doctors, and virtually every adult in my life who had any apparent authority. In no time at all, I had inferred that *everyone* knew me better than I knew myself!

Hard to believe someone could come to such a conclusion so quickly, right? Well, I think I arrived there within a few days of first hearing that simple, innocuous sentence. I'm sure Mom didn't intend it this way—she just wanted me to *behave!*

SELF-DENIAL SPIRAL

Unbeknownst to me, the moment I accepted Mom's proclamation, there followed in my young mind the gradual emergence of several inadvertent disempowering rules of conduct:

- I must look to others to know who I am.
- I must satisfy the needs of others before satisfying my own.
- I must do everything I can to make others happy.
- Everyone is more important than me.
- I'm not qualified to take care of myself.
- I'm not good enough.

These concepts found refuge in the dark recesses of my subconscious mind, but they soon congealed into beliefs that wielded enormous power everywhere in my life. Even when I held positive thoughts in my conscious awareness, these unconscious beliefs inevitably won out.

When I was 15, we gathered around the table one night for family dinner. My stepfather began grilling me about what I wanted to do with my life.

"A rock and roll musician!" I enthused. "I love playing guitar, and I'm already pretty good at it."

Mom rolled her eyes and shook her head. Stepdad took his cue. "Well, that does sound exciting." He snuck another glance at Mom before continuing. "But you know, David, for every successful musician, there are a million starving ones. And most musicians are addicted to drugs anyway. You don't want to end up like that, do you?"

What's amazing to me today is that I didn't even protest! All I managed was, "No, I guess you're right."

Over the next couple of years, I would test out different proposals to answer my stepdad's occasional queries. Only when I suggested *fighter pilot* did I receive anything resembling approval. Not surprising, since that is precisely what my stepfather was—a fighter pilot!

"Wonderful, sweetheart!" gushed Mom. Then came a patronizing stab to my heart. "You can always do your music as a hobby."

Deflated and effectively defeated, I caved in. Thus began my pattern of deference. The unconscious beliefs grew even stronger. I learned that if I wanted love and approval, I had to find ways to please everyone around me. Before long, I was living a life that appeared to be governed by a script I had no direct part in writing.

Meanwhile, in the background, shame, resentment, and anger were beginning to ferment. Like cancer.

BOTTOMING OUT

By the time I was 40, I had ticked all the initial boxes in the success checklist I believed society had created for me:

- Team-player and rule-observer: *Check.*
- High school and university education: *Check.*
- Steady job: *Check.*
- Wife and growing family: *Check.*
- House with moderate mortgage payment: *Check.*
- Contributing member of the community: *Check.*

By common metrics of the day, I was well on *The Path* to success and happiness. But I didn't feel happy; on the contrary, I was downright miserable. I had somehow devolved into an angry and resentful cynic—although I was firmly in denial about that for years! That is, until July 1992, following Mom's passing, when the dam burst and violent rage poured out of me...

"Hello?" she called. The door slammed behind her. "It's me!" My sister Diane and her daughter Bayley, unexpected visitors.

I looked up from the cutting board as she turned into the kitchen. "Hey, Di, what's up?"

"Bayley and I were heading home, and I just felt like checking in."

"Everything good here." I tilted my glass and took a swig. "Care for a martini? Glass of wine?"

"No," she said, "we're not staying. I just had something on my mind, and I wanted to talk to you."

Instantly on alert, I regarded her with curiosity and dread, waiting for a *Diane-bomb* to drop.

She blurted, "It's been three weeks since Mom died, and I still haven't seen you show any sadness. What the hell is wrong with you?"

My throat started burning as if a pressurized bottle of acid had burst within me. In the next moment, Diane was up against the wall, my right hand around her neck. In my racing mind, a thought screamed: *Don't you tell me how to grieve.* But what seethed out of my mouth was, "Don't you tell me how to be!"

Diane was so stunned that she hung motionless, gaping at me with wide eyes and open mouth. A distant part of my mind wondered: *How did this happen?* Then, complete silence, except for a distinct mental whisper: *Enough. Time to let go.*

Silence gave way to a strange wind rushing through my head. I regained awareness of the situation and released my hand. I shook my head absently and muttered, "I'm sorry, I don't know what. . ." The thought trailed off. Shame and horror rose in my chest to replace the overflowing acid.

Diane's face explored various expressions, settling on righteous indignation. Her body tensed. She glared at me and half-whispered-half-shouted: "How *dare* you!"

I was confused and disoriented. My body started shaking. Diane was clearly yelling other stuff at me, but nothing registered; I had mentally checked out.

Somehow, I found myself wandering aimlessly around the neighborhood. I replayed the scene in my mind multiple times, searching for comprehension. The dreadful realization dawned on me that my daughter, my son, and my niece had all witnessed my conniption. I cringed at the faint mental echoes of my daughter's plea: *Daddy, don't!*

By the time I ventured back home, Diane and Bayley were gone. So were my wife and children. They left me alone to stew in my own juices.

According to McLeod family dynamics back then, no one ever discussed this event—at least not around me. It was as if my tantrum never happened, and, indeed, I banished it from memory for years.

What a wake-up call! It forced me to take a serious look at my life, and I shuddered at what I saw: I had become a poster boy for the dysfunctional!

I knew I'd have to act soon or else risk my inner rage exploding again, causing serious and possibly irreversible damage to the people I loved most—my three children. Unfortunately, because I didn't understand what had gone wrong in my earlier life, I had no clue how to fix anything.

Repercussions rippled within me for three years. While I focused on completing my master's degree in Computer Science, I tried haphazardly to find support for what I needed to do. Eventually, I concluded that the help I sought was not available to me where I lived in Canada, so I made a radical and impetuous decision to change everything all at once. I terminated my PhD program, announced to my wife that I wanted a divorce, found a software engineering job in Silicon Valley, and left my family. In short, I fled what I believed was eating away at me from the inside out.

Alas, the misery I had been feeling did not simply disappear because of a change in venue. Indeed, shortly after arriving in Palo Alto, I began to experience severe depression that led to dark thoughts of suicide; it was only the bleak prospect of rendering my children fatherless that restrained me.

THE SACRED CARPET

Moving to California turned out to be the most beneficial decision I could have made. Serendipity connected me with resources that helped me uncover and heal hidden wounds that had spawned so much shame, pain, and anger within me over all those years. But the most profound healing and awakening came during a transformational weekend in May 2003, when I attended a *New Warrior Training Adventure.*

"This *Carpet* is sacred space." The facilitator stood in the center, circling slowly to address everyone. His manner was solemn and reverential.

"Many have come before you," he continued. "They stepped in, declared what they were here to do, and then broke themselves open to reveal—and to *seize*—the gold and the beauty within themselves. Today, if you choose, you can do the same."

A surge of excitement grew within me.

"This is serious work, perhaps the most important you will ever do. If you grab this opportunity, your life will change in ways you cannot even imagine right now." His words seemed to be directed right at me. He paused again. "You came here for a reason. Your mind might not know that reason, but your heart is certain you are here to reclaim something you left behind long ago."

Clearly, the facilitator revered the sacred space represented by *The Carpet.* Tears began to flow out of me.

"People have cried their eyes out on this *Carpet* to get what they came for. People have emptied their guts on this *Carpet* to get what they came for. People have cracked their hearts wide open on this *Carpet* to get what they came for. People have bled on this *Carpet* to get what they came for."

Another pause for effect. Then, barely above a whisper, he offered, "You can pass if you choose—and believe me, there is no shame in passing. I ask only that you let your heart make the choice, not your mind. For your heart knows the truth about who you really are and why you're here."

He had an air of reflection as he paced around, looking each man in the eye. "Who will be the first man on the *Carpet* today?"

As men stepped one-by-one into the sacred space, I became mesmerized. Each man took center stage, did some incredible healing work, and then, about 20 to 30 minutes later, marched off *The Carpet* transformed. It was beyond inspiring.

Then my turn came.

I stood in the center. The other men formed a perimeter of observers, and my body buzzed in anticipation. I was completely present, with no expectation and no agenda.

The facilitator appeared in front of me, and the men around the circle faded out of my awareness. He was a masterful guide, and I trusted him like I had trusted no one before. He asked questions to establish context, but their only real purpose was to get me to unlock emotions inside me that I had kept hidden away for so long.

And then it happened. The dormant volcano within me erupted, and hot, blood-red rage spewed out of me.

Screaming.

Cursing.

Raving.

A tennis racket magically appeared in my palm, which I immediately used to massacre a pile of pillows in front of me. But I did not see pillows! I saw Mother, Father, bosses, associates, priests, leaders, and yes, even God, all of whom I unconsciously held responsible for the deplorable state of my life. I pounded and raged until I had no more strength, until my voice was a hoarse whisper, until my breath was spent, until my inner volcano was empty.

I vaguely remember croaking that I just wanted someone to love me for who I am. From out of nowhere, a man came to my side to assume the role of *Ideal Mom*; he held me in the most loving way I could ever have imagined.

Tears flooded out me. My body shivered and shook with uncontrollable sobbing. *Ideal Mom* repeated phrases like "I love you so much" and "You are my amazing and beautiful boy." So much junk came out of my nose and eyes and mouth, I could not believe it!

Eventually, the deluge subsided, and I melted into *Ideal Mom's* arms. I was drained. I felt like a sponge that had been squeezed completely dry, and yet there was an unfamiliar profound peace within me. When I finally stood up, a surge of warm gold-blue light blossomed in my heart. I put my hands on my chest and smiled softly and effortlessly. I could not believe how amazing and alive I felt.

The facilitator faced me with a huge grin and asked a very simple question, "What is true about you right now, David, at this moment?"

Despite my raspy throat, I managed to declare, "I am a Divine being of boundless light and love, and I'm here to make the world a better place for everyone."

The men around the carpet burst into cheering and applause. Delicious gratitude flowed into my heart; fresh warm tears trickled down my cheeks. As I scanned the men's faces, my entire reality shifted. I felt immense love for everyone—including myself. I invoked a silent vow: *I will never again hide my feelings or my truth. No matter what happens in my life from now on, I will never again deny who I am to please anyone else.*

RIGHT TURN TO THE ON-RAMP

Transcendent Man? Me? Only God knows. But the events described here—and many others as well—have led me to my unique *path of transcendence.*

The Sacred Carpet brought forth a catharsis that shifted my entire life and alerted me to who I really am and why I am here. Since that experience, I have chosen to live according to a newfound mission: *to create universal harmony by modeling, fostering, and facilitating authentic magnificence.* A little lofty, perhaps, but it is a beacon that guides everything I do nowadays.

Life may not be perfect, but it's amazing, wonderful, and beautiful! I'm grateful to be alive, and thrilled to share insights with a world that I believe needs to hear them.

As you seek your own *path of transcendence,* consider this perspective:

You are not your name, your job description, your experiences, your thoughts, your feelings, or any of the roles you play in life. Those are merely *expressions* of your true nature! When you peel away superficialities, you'll discover that you are a magnificent and unlimited spiritual being of light and love, enjoying a temporary human experience on the physical plane. Recognize and remember the deepest truth of who you are, and live that truth in every single moment—without apology.

You'll be glad you did.

Fighter pilot. Best-selling author. Software engineer. Mentor. Aerobics instructor. Poet. Janitor. Lifeguard. Musician. Radio host. Graphics designer. Father. Student. Teacher. Photographer. Ordained minister. Yogi.

These roles—past and present—add up to a lot of life experience, which **David McLeod** brings to bear in his capacity as a transformational speaker, life-mastery coach, experiential facilitator, and writer/storyteller.

As a certified master life coach with a PhD in Metaphysical Sciences and a DD in Holistic Personal Coaching, David creates and shares powerful life mastery tools which enable adult men and women to transcend triggers, challenges, and obstacles so that they can express and experience the fullness of who they really are and thereby manifest truly magnificent and fulfilling lives.

Find out more about David and his offerings at:

https://yourlifemasterycoach.com

CHAPTER 14

REAWAKENING LOVE

A VOICE IN THE LIGHT

Patrick S. Fisher, Spiritual Coach

Faith and prayer have been my doctrine of outlet throughout a lifetime of hardship. Though, even I never really imagined hearing from God directly. Yet, in purely blissful, beautiful irony, that's exactly what transpired on the final night in which I called our elegant condo I shared with my wife home.

Within the downstairs walls of the upscale, modern condo, I prepared my makeshift bedroom for another painstaking evening. Couch converted to bed; I placed the sheets onto the cushions while once again preparing for another sleepless night. My friend, high-school sweetheart, and soon-to-be ex-wife and I were separated and awaiting the finalized documents of our divorce decree. Living in the same home in this egg-shelled situation felt like purgatory, and I was losing hope in everything once again. Yet despite the challenging circumstances, my ex and I still tried our best to maintain a sense of diplomacy for my precious young daughter, Rowan's sake.

Growing up in a family of dysfunction left a huge impact on how my life played out. Throughout my childhood, I never felt like I had a voice that was valued. This demoralizing realization came to me very early on that should I choose to use my voice, serious physical harm would engulf me. Taking me away like an endless storm on a dark, broken night. The fear I had for my father was not unfounded. I was wounded time and time again in ways a child should never have to endure. In countless ways, I felt so alone and wounded by this family dynamic and structure.

My father had three children with my birth mother, and I was the last of these three. He was a proud military drunk far before they even made their vows together. The night before their wedding in England, he nearly took his own life before it even really started. Coming home late with a drunken state of mind, he punched through their window while attempting to get back home. This would be just the first incident in a string of irrational, abusive behaviors in their marriage.

As my parents had their first child together in England, they came back to the states on assignment to Altus, Oklahoma, where my sister and I were both born in a military hospital. My first memories were all plagued by fear. Being a highly sensitive, empathic child, I was even more sensitive to the horrible things going on around me. I remember my father smashing glasses off the walls in a drunken rage. Over the crying children, "Get Out!" my mother would scream, as my father would scream back in sickening, uncontrollable rage, veins pulsating, his face becoming redder than Satan himself, he then turned to punch a hole in the wall. Unfortunately for him, the walls were solid, and he shattered his hand, requiring pins in his wrist and losing feeling in most of his fingers.

I do not blame my mother the first time she left, as she was pregnant by another man. It was very confusing to me, however, moving to Indiana and back and forth to New York. I loved my mother back then, and I was terrified of my father's mere existence. All the pain he held inside from their failed marriage left him with more ammunition to drink his life away. In a twisted fate, as my grandparents came to drive my two siblings and me again to Indiana, my mother's boyfriend was killed by a drunk driver. The irony in all of this cannot be overstated, as she chose to move to New York to be close to us along with her newly born child.

As time went by, I was embarrassed by my father's behavior in my childhood. Every single day he was drunk, and anytime he felt emotions, he went into fits of rage and physical abuse. As we eventually moved in with my mother in New York, my father lost his mind once again. Out of another unconsolable fit of rage, he again nearly killed himself. Accelerating erratically behind the wheel of his vehicle, completely intoxicated, he drove straight into a telephone pole. Once again, trying to end his own life and leaving his kids behind. Although he survived this suicide attempt, the damage was still done to his children. He would, however, take a keen sense of interest in helping to raise my half-brother.

Into my pre-teenage years, my father would watch all four of my mother's children, including her child from another man. Riding in the backseat of his cramped car, I found myself laughing at a joke my half-brother made. It was one of those jokes that keep getting funnier at every expression on your sibling's face. My father became annoyed at my small sense of happiness and threatened me twice, "You better stop laughing, or you'll be sorry." It was one of those moments where the humor was more powerful than his evil threats. I continued to try to stop laughing. I even put a hand over my mouth to try and stop. But after a few minutes, I thought about the joke again and laughed. I signed my own beating warrant. He pulled over the car, opened up the door, and began beating me with his fists until I cried. He shut the door and continued driving again. "There, I bet you don't think it's funny anymore, do you?! He laughed so menacingly like his highest glory was beating out any happiness from me. I continued to cry in the back as I cowered over from the pain in my stomach, hiding away but wishing to disappear for good.

On another occasion, my two siblings and I were arguing in the car. This was in the summertime, and my father's logical response—he locked us in that car with the heat and forced us to stay inside there. It was one of those moments where you were so scared, and all you could do was pray. It wasn't as bad as the times when he would choke my sister and me unconscious in the bathroom. Or as bad as the time when he beat me publicly after a poor performance in a middle school basketball game. Yet none of that was as painful as the words of an uncaring mother.

Heading into the door of my mother's home, I could tell she was angry. The one thing I craved as a child was my mother's love, yet her own childhood left her emotionless. "Did you change over the laundry?" she asked. "No, I forgot. I'm sorry," I replied. This sent her into a rant that left me feeling even more sorry for having to do something. "I'm sorry, I love you, Mom," I said. "I don't love you, Patrick," She replied. This response ripped out my heart. As I went down into the unfinished basement where my bed was under the stairs, I turned instead into the heap of soiled clothing. I laid in them and cried. It was the first time as a child that I really felt dirty. It was also the first time that I actually wanted to die.

That's just the way things went in my childhood. I began to rebel and just wanted to escape. Books became a world where I could imagine myself somewhere else. Envisioning a family that truly loved me was something I was so desperate for. I would lay awake at night praying in all my childhood innocence, "Dear God, if there truly is a magical school like Hogwarts, please, Lord, rescue me and send me there ."I wanted so badly to escape this life of pain and sorrow.

The level of childhood trauma I endured left me needing to escape. My brother enlisted into the Army by my parents at 17, and my sister left even earlier at just 16 years of age. The abuse they suffered left my brother emotionless and my poor sister with severe emotional instability. The Doctor diagnoses mental illness, but in reality, we just grew up in a life of true hell. Love was as foreign of a concept to us as any foreign language, really. When I was 15, I too left the home of my mother again. I was sent to my elderly grandparents' home to live after another volatile fight with my mother's new husband. This was one of the greatest blessings in disguise to me at the time. I needed the love of my grandmother, Rose, who was truly the only person I knew that ever showed me love. She was a woman of true faith—a healer, an intuitive, and a wise woman full of love and discernment.

When I moved into my grandparent's lifelong home, it was also the place where my father lived. I walked into my newly appointed room upstairs, across the hall from where he stayed. There wasn't much in the room at that time, and my bed was simply a foldable cushioned cot to be laid on the ground. Taking in this new environment, all I could truly feel was sadness and desolation. Taken out of my school for the third time in a year, I laid down on my little cot. Feeling totally isolated with my life changing instantly. I cried myself to sleep that night. Wishing once again to escape from the world I was thrust into.

Heading into my Senior year, I moved schools again, but I also enlisted into the US Military for post-graduation. The year went by quickly, and as soon as June hit, I graduated and prepared to depart. Heading into the large gates and military post, a Drill Instructor boarded the bus, "Get off and Shut Your Mouths!" "Stay in Line!", "We own you now!" I smiled inwardly at this familiar sound of screaming chaos as we began the journey of losing who we were and finding a newfound strength and voice.

Coming back to my small Washington DC apartment after deploying to Haiti, I was feeling very defeated inside. I lived in a very poor building where the metal can bonfires and fallen memorials littered the sidewalks. This was the place that began my journey into spiritual warfare. Seeing the children of Haiti with no limbs, facial burns, and no place to call home was devastating. The scars they bore equally were expressed in the scars left by those that treated them. I wanted to scream at people who complained over small things. *How can you be so insensitive when others are struggling so badly somewhere in the world?*

Breaking karma and trauma left in family bloodlines can seem overwhelming. I took on this challenge headfirst. I vowed to love my daughter and to show her a softer feminine side, which I had never witnessed growing up. I began going to therapy, pursuing my education, and learning to express myself creatively. After eight years on Active Duty and two years in the reserves, I left the military for my beautiful daughter Rowan's sake. I knew I wanted to be in her special life and that she needed me. The same spiritual gifts I have, equally are hers by divine birthright. She is very empathic, intuitive, and a natural leader, clearly pointing to her higher state of consciousness and morality. Her mom and I strive to encourage her self-expression through art, singing, nature, and encouraging her to have that powerful inner voice speak. This is beyond important spiritually, as it allows our ancestors to be at peace knowing their mistakes have been paid in full.

Laying down on the couch feeling transparently sad, I began thinking about my life. Everything moved so quickly as we awaited the divorce paperwork from the courts. As I lay on the couch in quiet reflection, the one thing that was clear was this chapter was finally done. Out of nowhere, I heard this ground-shaking, magnificent voice come through in my mind. The voice was like sheer power mixed with absolute love. The consistency is hard to express, so I will do my best to explain God's voice. He came through striking trepidation and a level of love in me that I have never felt in this lifetime. God said, *I command you to go forth and preach and teach the Gospel!"* Where should I go?" I asked. *They will come to you,* God replied. The power of God's Divine Masculine voice, mixed with his pure, loving essence, left me crying and fearful. If I knew then that God was going to speak to me, I would have been ready with a whole list of things to say. I feel ashamed now that I didn't even tell him thank you or just how much I truly love and adore him and his heavenly kingdom. When God spoke to me, he didn't ask me if I would like to do this. It was not in some question form or passive inquiry. His power is unquestioned, and I am honest when

I say I truly do fear God. At the same time, just to have his gaze on me directly and to hear his unbelievably powerful voice still invokes tears in my eyes every time I recount God's beautiful essence.

Hearing God's message left me feeling confirmed in my already inner knowing of his existence. Prophets are chosen by God's all-knowingness, and his confirmation in his son Jesus's death for us all changed me forever. You may think that confirming my beliefs may push me to negate others' chosen beliefs. That could not be farther from the truth. Hearing God's message sent me on a mission to learn about other cultures. It made me want to connect with all walks of life and to learn from one another through a lens of love. The experience left me humbled and did not in any way make me feel egotistical, or the "I told you so." Know that is ignorance; it is not the way of love we all desperately need in our lives for this current time of spiritual healing as a collective. My understanding as an intuitive is that since God spoke to me, surely, he speaks to his prophets from all faiths. Jesus welcomed and loved God's children in every form. He did not use religion to cause separations but rather shows his example of universal love in his willingness to die and be tortured for us all.

Shortly after moving out of our condo and into my apartment, I began going through a spiritual awakening. For three days, I felt like I was actually dying without leaving this world and body behind. At night I would cry as physical burns appeared from the shedding away of this person I was never meant to become. I would drive to this local cemetery and sit in contemplation. Because of the level of pain I was in, I could no longer tell if I was dead or alive. I needed to witness the tombstones of the dead and focus on the reality that I was, in fact, still living. The process of enlightenment is painful, but it also pushes us to the place where we are able to help and heal others. My friends began to notice the changes instantly. "Patrick, you are glowing!" My one friend told me after not seeing me for a few weeks. It was releasing all of the pain from my life while finding my voice to finally express myself! It felt so liberating to stop caring what others think and felt about me.

My heart began to beat again as new life poured through me. My rebirth left me different in many ways. My energies evolved as my spiritual gifts arose to the forefront of my life. I began finding myself reawakening to what love is. As I recorded songs, wrote poems, short stories, and performed

Tarot for clients, I was actually healing my own heart. For the first time in a long time, I began following my passions and allowed my creative abilities to shine through. Channeling waves of love from the angelic realm, I began healing at an extremely fast rate. Being surrounded by all of these loving, supportive spiritual beings left me feeling youthful, beautiful, and radiant. I made self-love my literal job of sorts. Everything from starting a blog, connecting to people all around the globe, and inspiring activism all blossomed simply by being myself. The inner child self that always wanted to come forth, blossom, and be seen and heard. That voice I heard from God allowed my spiritual authority to pour out. I noticed when I spoke, people stopped and listened. I noticed when I showed them my heart that they were so eager to want theirs healed as well. I started an online community where I am able to welcome all walks of life into a safe space.

Coming out spiritual can be a daunting task indeed. As I began to show my abilities to channel my guides, it garnished a mix of reactions. Some felt uneasy at my ability to read them, but I always ensure my clients that I read messages from a place of love, healing, and support. In the same sense, I found a universal connection with all walks of life, which allows me to open my heart to all. As I walked away from the family that once was allowed to abuse me, I established boundaries for the first time in my life. I inspire others by showing them that you do not need to be somebody's doormat or punching bag. I use my voice to motivate others through positivity, healing, spiritual alignment, and faith. Those clients drawn to me should anticipate healing, feeling more inspired, and loving themselves on a much higher scale. I seek to inspire a renewal of faith, a rekindled spirit, and a life of meaning in all of the beautiful souls that seek to be set free.

Patrick S. Fisher, Spiritual Coach, is a source of healing and inspiration for coaching clients. After a decade of work with the Armed Forces and the US Government, Patrick attended Suny Adirondack College, followed by Siena College, an English Major, and Religious Studies Minor. He found himself through deep meditation, cultural studies, and an openness to come out spiritual in order to share his gifts with the world.

After launching a successful Life Coaching Business and blog, Patrick began using his spiritual gifts of healing, Clairvoyance, Clairaudience, and discernment to help clients find answers. With over a decade of experience in Biblical studies, Numerology, Astrology, and Tarot, Patrick has found that using a combination of spirituality and self-love is key to transformation. He creates short stories, writes on spiritual topics, and is an activist for promoting change and ascending to a more loving world.

Patrick has the ability to channel wisdom and guidance from the higher realms in order to guide clients. Setting a clear vision, he helps clients find their inner voice and set meaningful goals every step of their personal journey.

He is a visionary in his peaceful approach, allowing clients to truly open up and find those hidden talents and passions that change the trajectory of life.

Connect with Patrick:

Website: Spiritual Healing and Self-love guidance – Spiritual Blog (wordpress.com) Patrickfisher333.wordpress.com

E-mail: Ps12fish@icloud.com

Links to Social Media:

Facebook: https://www.facebook.com/profile.php?id=100079704319414

LinkedIn: https://www.linkedin.com/in/patrick-fisher-all-are-welcome-in-my-community-🙏👍-blessed-055574180/

Instagram: @Patrickfisher1234 TikTok: @Patrickfisher243

CHAPTER 15

WHEN YOUR SOUL CALLS

FOLLOWING THE THREAD TO YOUR LIFE'S PURPOSE

Mark J. Platten, MBA

MY STORY

"What would you teach tomorrow if you were to teach anything? Don't think about it, just say it out loud," my wife Ahriana asked.

"Men's work" dropped out of my mouth and shocked me, wishing I could rewind and say something else. Had I taken the time to think about it, men's work wouldn't have made the top ten, so I knew it was extremely important to pay attention to what had come from a deeper place within.

My wife and I were on our way back from a self-designed retreat in Taos, New Mexico, where we contemplated what we wanted to do in the next phase of our lives. It was September of 2020, and Covid slowed me down enough to realize my work was getting in the way of what my soul was asking of me...even though I wasn't sure what that was. It was surprising to realize I had fallen into the trap of contentment instead of following my inner guidance. My work as faculty at Colorado State University completely wooed me into believing I made it, whatever that meant. I became acutely aware there was something more important to do.

We spent the first several days in Taos talking about how our transition would look and feel. Ahriana was retiring from her career as a minister, our youngest was in college, and we had time to focus on ourselves for the first time in 20 years. We wanted to slow down, have more quality time with each other, invest in friendships, make a difference, and travel the world.

After several days of brainstorming, Ahriana said, "I'm feeling called to create a course on ceremonies for ministers. It's needed, and I've had so many ministers ask if I'd teach this course that it feels like the right thing for me to do."

Part of me hoped we'd find something to teach together, but once she decided, I turned my focus on what I wanted individually. I was still not sure several days later when "men's work" fell out of my mouth.

Following your soul's calling or purpose is something that a lot of people talk about but few pursue. Growing up on the farm connected me deeply to the earth. Thirty years of meditation, shamanic drumming/journeying, dreamwork, ceremonies, and spiritual quests into nature have helped me develop a deep relationship with Spirit. It has always communicated with me, pulling me forward as though guided by something beyond myself. I receive messages through sensing, hearing, feeling, dreaming, or knowing when the Divine communicates with me. There is a subtle difference between it and my ego, and its guidance is always for my highest good. Even when I initially don't want to follow it, I yield once I get my mind out of the way. When it comes across as either lifting me up on a pedestal or shaming me, I know I'm not connected to the Sacred. It can be firm or supportive, but there is always a sense of detachment, where the choice is mine, and it's providing insight and guidance.

My 54th birthday, November 29, was two months away. I knew for over 25 years that something significant would happen this year. I didn't know what, only that it would be positive and necessary for my growth into the next phase of my life. The process of considering what I would do next at Taos was more than an exercise; it was critical to entering the year of expansion that had haunted me for decades.

In 2004 I started a Ph.D. in Men's Divinity. It was totally outside what I had done, but the calling was strong. I traveled across Colorado, interviewing men's groups and reading the top men's books. After all the research, I realized I was missing the deeper, inner work of leading a men's group. I started a small one in Colorado Springs and, after a couple of months, was asked by one of the men if I would talk to the lead minister at Unity Church in the Rockies about starting a men's group.

"I'm curious why you're interested in starting a men's group," I asked Reverend Palmer?

"As strange as it may seem, it's the women who approached me and pleaded with me to start a men's group so their husbands can experience the same sort of closeness the women's group does!"

I laughed, "Of course they did. It can be challenging to get men to connect unless it's around drinking or sports. Let's put together a series of opportunities that engage the physical and spiritual at the same time."

We met every two weeks over nine months, focusing on the exterior world through experiences such as sweat lodge, drumming, hiking, and ceremony. Over 30 men attended consistently, and there was tremendous growth and connection between us. I laughed at one of the participants who told me, "You're the only Sagittarius I've ever learned anything from." I took it as a compliment. After the first course, I had their trust, and we spent the following nine months going to the interior world, looking at death, loss, wounds, dreams, wounds with our fathers, fatherhood, childhood, and the realm of the Lover archetype. It was rich and rewarding to experience men's vulnerability, openness, and heart-centered support and connection.

At the end of the second course, I was guided to turn the program over to the men so they could share their gifts instead of relying on me. Shortly thereafter, I heard, *Windancer, It's time for you to put the men's work on hold. You don't have grey hair, your children are young, and your father is still alive. There will come a time when you are called upon to engage with men again, but for now, it would be wise to let it rest.*

That was it. I knew it was true to the core of my being. I stepped away from the men's group, quit the Ph.D. program, and stopped my pursuit of men's work. So, when "men's work" dropped out of my mouth on the way back from Taos, it was extremely significant, and I wasn't sure I was up for the task. I have gray hair, have navigated raising five boys, but gratefully, my father is still alive. Perhaps that's what bothered me, that I hadn't met all the criteria Spirit had given me 15 years earlier, and I would lose my father if I continued.

Eventually, I realized the guidance was for my highest good and yielded. Just as I had laid down the men's work 15 years prior, I took up the torch with renewed vigor, gathered all the new men's books (again, not much there), researched online men's courses, social media sites, blogs, websites, and podcasts related to men. I found a lot of focus on four areas: warrior energy, money, health/fitness, and sex. I have a lot of experience with Carl Jung's work, including the King, Magician, Warrior, and Lover archetypes used in many men's and shadow work training. The courses I came across were primarily in the realm of the Warrior.

I paid attention to the challenges men were encountering. What I found was many of them in my age demographic were having difficulty finding a good relationship. They wondered why they constantly called in the same type of person in a different body and couldn't find the "one." Based on that information, I created my first course, Finding Love After Heartache, A Man's Roadmap for Creating a Lasting Relationship. I attended a course for creating online programs and received overwhelmingly positive feedback, with almost 100 attendees telling me how necessary this was for men. It was the confirmation I was on the right path.

My 54th birthday came clearly into view as we entered November, and I received another message from Spirit. *To bring your fullest self to this work, you'll have to exhume the shadow parts of yourself that you've done such a good job of keeping contained since childhood. You could do the work without integrating those parts, but it will be a shallow, veneer version, and you won't reach your full potential.*

I had spent the previous three years researching the subconscious and how it controls 95% of our cognitive function, according to recent research from Harvard and MIT. I was aware there were parts of myself the subconscious isolated to protect me when I was a child, and I knew if I didn't bring those parts out of the shadows and integrate them into my adult self, I would continue living a partial life.

I dug in but could only get so far before hitting what felt like a steel plate in my subconscious that I couldn't get through or around. It felt threatened by my desire to let the shadow parts out and was one of the strangest sensations I've ever felt. I knew where I needed to go, yet my subconscious was stopping me from going there. I needed help.

Like many men, asking for help meant I had somehow failed. Of course, this is the toxic message I'd been fed since a young boy. To be anything other than a lone wolf was not being a real man. It was humbling, and I felt exposed reaching out to friends, asking if they knew anyone they would recommend. Karin came up from three people, so I felt she was the one. I held a preliminary meeting to make sure it was a good match, and she seemed to have the skills and credentials to get past my shields. I was ready to embark on the shadow work process. Then she told me the price.

I had an idea of what I thought the cost of the six sessions would be, but I was off by a factor of four! I don't know if she felt my shock, and I tried to play it off like money was no issue, but inside I was screaming: *Are you kidding me? That's insane. Do you know what I could do with that amount of money? Maybe this is a message that I can do this by myself after all.*

"Sounds good, but I'll have to talk to my wife and get back to you," I said, knowing I could use her as the reason to say no.

Ahriana reinforced my shock, although she said she would support me if it felt like the right thing. I meditated on it, and something unexpected happened: my heightened emotions around asking for help and the issue of cost dissolved. I entered a profound state of stillness and surrender, and I knew then my subconscious was on board. I'm not sure exactly what happened, but I believe my Higher Self collaborated with my subconscious to understand what we would gain with the shadow work.

It was an emotionally charged process of resurrecting core parts of my being and reintegrating them into my adult self. It was wrought with screams, tears, re-lived pain, fear, uncertainty, anxiety, and exhaustion. It also awakened tears of deep love, a lightening of my being, recapturing inner power and confidence, and the certainty of self-love. My shadow parts were not my worst parts that needed hiding, but the deepest, truest aspects of myself I'd been living without most of my life! It was liberating, and I felt like a new person. I was ready.

I developed the course with passion and drive, working until almost midnight after work and through the weekends. I began marketing and held four webinars to drive enrollment. I planned the launch for February 14, the perfect timing for a program about relationships. And then I hit a wall. I created a series of Facebook marketing ads, which were pulled because they thought I was selling sex toys! It took me almost two weeks of appeals to convince them that my product had nothing to do with sex toys, at least not directly.

With these challenges, I decided to make it a free course and invited the participants to donate at the end if they found it valuable. When February 14 arrived, I launched to one person, my best friend. It was a total bust. In retrospect, it made a lot of sense why most men's programs focus on the Warrior archetype because it's about the physical realm and the easiest to access for most men. It was clear that I would need to start in one of these areas, gain their trust, and then move into the emotional courses.

Demoralized, I was exhausted and not sure why Spirit had led me through that process. One of the things I've realized about the information coming from the Divine is sometimes it's not obvious why I'm guided to do something. The research I conducted led to offers for numerous men's programs over social media. The day after I put my course on hold, I came across one that looked almost exactly like what I had created: capped at 100 men, framed in the four Jungian archetypes, focused on the full man, based on small groups within the larger group, and was priced at $500 instead of the typical $497. As I dug deeper, I was impressed and joined their 12-week program, which started in July 2020. Perhaps I wasn't supposed to run my course but had been guided to participate in this program instead.

The only thing that worried me about the course was that it was led by two former military special forces men, who focused a lot of their promotion to the military, police, firefighters, and EMS professions. Although I spent seven years as an Air Force officer, I hadn't been in that sort of ultimate masculine energy for a very long time. In all honesty, I believed many in those professions hadn't moved past the young Warrior male energy of "kill it or fuck it," and I was worried I wouldn't be able to connect with them. I was wrong.

Each week, we shared what we learned from the lesson and our "gold" and "shadow." It was an environment of men being vulnerable with one another and finding great strength and acceptance through our wounds, addictions, and failures. This was antithetical to what we'd been taught a real man was supposed to be in the world. It has been the greatest disservice to men, believing we could figure it all out on our own, that we could protect, create our empires, rule the work environment, be a great father, always know the answer, and be Casanova in the bedroom. It has set us up for failure. Not only to others but also to ourselves because we know where we've failed the code. We think others have what it takes, but somehow, we're inadequate. We have not given ourselves the grace of failure where we discover compassion for humanity as we recognize ourselves in the eyes of others. This deep sharing was freeing as we set down the baggage of manhood we had been sold, realizing it wasn't ours to carry.

It was toward the middle of the program that a subtle shift occurred. I went from being one of the participants in the group to someone sought out for advice and guidance. I realized I was older than most by about a decade, which is the first time I've had that experience in a men's group. Once I recognized this, there was an energetic shift within me, where I became a guide and mentor rather than a teacher. It may seem a trivial difference, but it was life-changing for me. It locked in the piece that was missing when Spirit said I was not ready to continue with the men's work. It required me to shift my energy and how I related and connected with men. It was powerful, and Ahriana said it was so dramatic that it took her several months to get used to it.

At the end of the program, we held an awards ceremony where the 120 participants voted for men who demonstrated characteristics in seven categories. I received the most coveted award, The Man In Full, which demonstrates maturity and fulfillment in each of the King, Magician, Warrior, and Lover archetypes. I have received over 50 national and state awards at the collegiate level, but this award meant more than all of those. It was not based on what I thought about myself or what I had accomplished but on what my peers experienced from me throughout the program. I wanted to give back, so I became a co-leader in the next course for one of the 8-10 men roundtables, coaching them through the process I had just finished. With that, I knew I was complete with the program.

My 55th birthday happened just before the end of that leadership stint, and with it, the closure of the year of my life I'd been waiting 25 years to discover what it would bring. I imagined wealth, fame, prestige, or being a best-selling author. What I found was not as grandiose on the exterior but much more profound overall. I listened to the call from Spirit as "men's work" spilled out of my mouth. I followed the thread to develop the course and heeded the voice that invited me to step into a fuller version of myself by exhuming the shadow parts. I used my course failure as an opportunity to look wider instead of giving up and was guided to the King of the Four Houses (K4) men's program.

It was there that I healed a rift in my belief that only spiritual men had the presence and ability to be vulnerable. My world opened to see all men as part of the brotherhood who are all struggling with the same things, regardless of profession, religion, or political position, opening my heart and mind to my own biases where I believed myself better than the others. I found a deep love for a segment of men in society whom I wouldn't choose to spend any time with previously, and in that, I expanded my heart and put down my shields. The final gift was the shift into a new dimension of my being, where I became a mentor and guide to help men develop their integral selves and become men in full.

Mark J. Platten has his soul rooted in nature, in the holy and sacred communion with the Earth and Cosmos. His drive lies in helping people find their passion, purpose, and path through developing the integral human and connecting them to nature. He integrates brain science, indigenous wisdom, rites/rituals/ceremonies, connection with nature, and the practical application in the physical realm to become the best version of ourselves.

He is the founder of Integral Human Initiative and Integral Man Institute and helps men and women align with their highest selves through Jungian archetypes, the four subtle bodies (physical, mental, emotional, and spiritual), and working with the subconscious to support our highest possibilities.

Mark's bestselling book, *The Art of Connecting With Nature,* is an anthology of 22 co-authors sharing how they connect with nature through various rites, rituals, ceremonies, and practices. You can find author interviews on his YouTube channel below and information about courses, rituals, and ceremonies on his website.

He is also an author in the Amazon bestselling anthology, *Shaman Heart: Turning Pain Into Passion and Purpose* as well as an international award-winning Haiku writer.

On the academic/professional side, Mark has an MBA in Organizational Management, served seven years as an Air Force officer, taught natural resources at the collegiate level, traveled internationally for 16 years as the lead environmental specialist for a company out of London, and since 2008, has been faculty at Colorado State University.

You can connect with him on the following sites:

Websites: www.markjplatten.com

Integral Human Initiative: www.integralhumaninitiative.com

Integral Man Institute www.integralmaninstitute.com

Facebook pages:

https://www.facebook.com/TheArtofConnectingWithNature

https://www.facebook.com/whennaturespeaks

https://www.facebook.com/IntegralManInstitute

YouTube for The Art of Connecting With Nature author interviews:

https://www.youtube.com/channel/UCQVjtyoGFr25I8xrz2dGQ8A

YouTube for Integral Man Institute:

https://www.youtube.com/channel/UCZ-eLsxRb8wAQ2FqfRO7t4g

You can contact Mark via email at markjplatten@gmail.com

CHAPTER 16

EMBRACING THE NOW

RELEASING "SHOULDS" TO REALIZE UNLIMITED POSSIBILITY

Shervin Hojat, Ph.D.

When I think of somebody living in the present moment, my mother comes to mind—my mother in her later years, when she had dementia. She was solidly in the "now," as though held by an invisible anchor. Yet, she was light as well, like a butterfly freed from the burden of both past and future.

When she turned her focus in my direction during that time, I felt her love and attention, completely free from judgment. The veil of "shoulds" that once existed between us was no more. Her smile was slow to arrive and slow to leave, unlike the flashing half-smiles she had for me in the past. We shared simple meals, her favorite at Panda Express, like two old friends. We laughed and communicated soul-to-soul.

Like a couple of kids, we walked through department stores, and I took her pictures as she modeled different hats and sunglasses. Finally, after so many years, I felt it was okay to be myself in my mother's company. It was okay to be playful. And it was apparent that my mother felt safe letting her inner child come out to play as well. We finally saw each other through a lens of love: *I see your beauty.*

Those experiences with my mother helped me answer a question I had since childhood: *Why are so many old people happy, even though they know they may die soon?* Freed from her past and from her future, my mother was trusting the *now,* the only time she had and the only time we all have—*right now.* People teetering on the edge of death (many of them) smile and enjoy life because they know that now is the time to experience joy. They trust now, and they trust life.

I began to trust life, too, although the process was impeded somewhat as I struggled to accept that my mother was not as strong or as perfect as I had always found her. I was clinging to that story created by me in the past! I was dragging that story into the now. But eventually, I began to follow her lead and trust life, too. I began spending more and more time in the now.

I would not have imagined that one of the most important moments in my life would be at my mother's side, holding her hand while she was taking her last breaths. I realized I was about to lose my mother, the biggest supporter, and nurturer I had ever known. My newfound trust in life enabled me to be strong and loving enough to support her peaceful transition. As the monitor showed her heartbeat slowing, as her breathing pattern became irregular, I squeezed her hand and gently whispered in her ear, "Mom, I love you. You are safe. Go to the light. Your mom and sister are waiting for you."

To me, trusting life means doing my best and accepting the results without resistance and drama. We don't always know why things happen or why we get one result instead of another. But worry is just a troublesome story about the future, and it takes us away from the present moment. In truth, outcomes are often much better than we could ever imagine. I have learned I must simply do my best in the now and let the future take care of itself.

LOST TO "SHOULDS"

Once, while attending tango class, I saw a woman across the room practicing walking, the foundation of the dance. Only after mastering the walk can we enter the dance with elegance. Her eyes met mine with a smile. I felt something unique and mysterious in her energy. I wasn't romantically drawn to her, just inexplicably interested. *Who is she? What makes her stand out? Why is she taking this class?* I wanted to get to know her better over a cup of coffee.

I was driving home after class when a thought so sudden and new stopped me in my tracks. My mind was racing. *Why don't I have such interest and curiosity in myself? Why don't I want to get to know myself over a cup of coffee?*

At a young age, I was told—both implicitly and explicitly—what I should like and what I should do. Many of those things were not in line with my interests, curiosity, and passions. I learned to obey. I learned that if I continued to rebel, I would do so at a high cost. My interpretation was that I—*who I really am*—was not important, likable, or interesting. And because, as a child, I depended on others for my very survival, I conformed to the "shoulds" and became interested in knowing and pleasing others at the expense of knowing my own likes, dislikes, and passions.

As a result, I struggled even as an adult to know myself. I avoided being alone, first because I did not know myself and second, perhaps worse, because I learned not to be curious about myself. Why would I want to be alone when "alone" left me in the company of a disinterested stranger? I was lost to the long shadow of "shoulds." Maybe you can relate. I had no clue what I wanted or what my purpose was. I knew I wanted the people around me, including my parents and friends, to appreciate and like me. Although they gave me guidelines, such as, "Study and do well at school," such advice did not tell me how to live happily.

At age 44, as I was getting older, I began a quest to find the secret, or secrets, to a happy life. I looked to family and friends for an example of happiness and peace of mind, but I didn't see the happiness of the sort I wanted. Instead, I saw others trying to conform, much the way I had always done. Many of my "successful" coworkers seemed unhappy as well. Some worked long hours to avoid life at home; others lived for Friday when they could escape work. Nobody seemed to have the answer to my question: *Where is the path to happiness?*

Instead of discovering that path, I discovered many different paths to unhappiness. I began to observe what *not* to do and patterns of thought *not* to repeat. I saw that one week of vacation happiness meant very little next to the other 51 weeks when I felt partially dead. And I realized I needed to find or create my own happiness. Nobody, not even my spouse or children, could make me happy.

LOST TO THE PAST AND FUTURE

During this time of mindful observation, I noticed in myself a habit of clinging to the past. This habit, like the habit of abandoning myself, came from early-life experiences and observations. As a child and teenager, I witnessed my parents blaming each other for things that happened years prior, things they insisted caused their present unhappiness. Their stories about the past kept them from enjoying the present moment and put distance between them, further feeding their unhappiness. Witnessing these conflicts affected me deeply, and I believe they planted a seed of misunderstanding: Unhappiness can be explained by looking to the past.

Later, as an adult, I observed my own habit of clinging to the past and came to realize I was losing happiness to the past—more specifically, to the stories I told myself about the past. I clung to my stories of past hurts as a way to explain or justify present-day resentment and bitterness. I clung to stories about bad things that happened and to stories about good things that happened but ended. Sadly, every time I repeated those stories, they were strengthened, becoming part of my unhappy identity. It was a treacherous and painful cycle.

Likewise, I observed that I was losing happiness to the future—specifically, to the stories I was telling myself about the future. When I lost my job at age 52, I was fearful and worried about my family's financial security and the future. Again, worry is an example of a bad story made up about the future. Obviously, stories about the future can also be good, such as when we create a vision for ourselves. But even the visioning practice can contribute to unhappiness if we focus on what we do not have in the present moment, in other words, if we focus on lack.

I came to see that in order to be happy, I had to let go of my stories about the past and my stories about the future. Clinging to those stories prevented me from showing up in the present moment with compassion, empathy, and gratitude. Those stories limited the potential of the present moment. I set an intention to consciously create my experience *in the now*, the only time we actually have. Once I released those chattering stories, replacing them with heartfelt gratitude, my mind and spirit were free to experience joy and peace. If my clinging sounds familiar—if it's something that you engage in as well—I recommend noticing the habit and gently redirecting your mind to the present moment.

BEFRIENDING MYSELF

I determined that I wanted to know myself and acknowledged that now was the only time I could do it. I became determined to stay in the now and to discover myself right where I was. Like most new things, my commitment to knowing myself felt very awkward at first. How do I start a conversation with a stranger? I started small: *What are my favorite colors? Why am I feeling tense?* I did my best to pose these questions and to welcome the answers with genuine care. Then I brought my curiosity closer to the heart. When I was feeling sad, a feeling I would have judged as weakness in the past, I responded by acknowledging my sadness and investigating its primary source. Instead of feeling frustrated and condemned by my own judgments, I now felt heard, supported, and acknowledged.

As I practiced caring for myself, I began posing deeper questions about my own spirituality and spiritual belief system. *Does this idea meet my needs? Does it bring me peace and joy?* When the answer was "yes," I entered the ideas more deeply. When the answer was "no," I continued my search. Regardless of the answer, I remained kind, curious, and self-respecting. I became truly interested in myself in the present moment.

DEVELOPING INTUITION AND LIVING AUTHENTICALLY

As I became happier, I began to see that my life did include other happy people! I wondered whether this newly observed happiness had always been there imperceptible to me, but I didn't dwell on the question. Instead, I started focusing on characteristics in others that I wanted to cultivate in myself.

I adored people who could use their intuition and psychic ability to solve problems. With this insight, I began to follow their example. I saw that intuition is a form of knowing, like GPS at a crossroads. To avail me of more information and data and to continue making better decisions in the life of my new friend (myself), I started improving my own intuition by using my intuition. Over time, my confidence in my intuition improved until I trusted myself more than I trusted the opinions of others.

I continued to show more curiosity and kindness toward myself by fearlessly listening to my intuition without judgment, and I began to trust my intuition more and more. I even shared my intuition about others in psychic and Reiki classes. I received positive feedback and gained more confidence. My improved self-regard and my growing intuition fed one another, creating a positive cycle. I saw myself becoming more myself.

As I got to know myself, I moved toward greater authenticity. To live authentically, we must be willing to discover how we feel and what our needs are—rather than denying our feelings and needs by saying "All is well," or "It does not matter." Imagine if you told your friend about a struggle or a longing and your friend said, "Ignore those feelings. Behave as if everything is fine." Would you continue to share authentically or deeply with that friend? Would you trust a person who advised you to be dishonest? Not if you want to live authentically in the present moment! This is why my own friendship was so important as I moved toward a happy life.

Authenticity doesn't require simply knowing what we think, feel, and need. To live authentically, we must also *express* those thoughts, feelings, and needs. Self-expression like this—*authentic* self-expression—requires vulnerability, which is often misperceived as weakness, especially for men. In truth, authentic self-expression is a sign of courage and confidence because it requires risk, the risk of rejection.

When we refuse to live authentically, we betray ourselves. The reverse is also true: when we strive to be authentic, we honor ourselves. That is what I hope for you, that you can take the risk to honor yourself. For me, this has resulted in more self-confidence, self-respect, and self-empathy. It has resulted in greater happiness. I do my best to live fully in the present moment and to value authenticity more than I fear judgment or rejection: fear is just a negative story about the future! I make a better choice.

USING MY GIFTS TO FULFILL MY PURPOSE

As I began to live authentically and honor myself, I expressed myself in new ways by sharing my feelings and insights through writing and poetry. I became comfortable with writing—something I had hated in high school. I developed a practice of reflecting deeply on my day-to-day life experience and sharing those reflections via my bi-weekly blog, a practice I've continued for 14 years. In 2008, I published my first book, titled *Tend to Your Garden Within.* This book documents my questions, insights, and observations over the years. I published my second book, a collection of poetry titled *Symphony of My Heart,* in 2019.

Although I initially hesitated to share my intimate thoughts and feelings with the world, I became aware of my family's history, my own ancestral history, which involved repressing emotions. I wanted to rewrite this history, and—through my intuition, authenticity, and writing—I have accomplished this goal.

I also discovered within myself an urge to paint, another thing I hated when I was younger. My first painting was my dog, Tiber, a toy poodle who was my daily companion for four years while I was working from home. With my first painting behind me, I felt free to express myself through paintings. I then painted animals, birds, and scenes that inspired me. The painting practice helped me later on when I started doing nature photography, something I still enjoy and cherish tremendously.

I have studied Silva mind control, dream interpretation, shamanism, Reiki, fingerprint reading, conscious language, eye reading, Enneagram, John Maxwell coaching training, Cards of Destiny, meditation, and self-discovery through silence. All of these modalities have been very beneficial to my personal and spiritual growth.

Cards of Destiny is a self-discovery tool I often use and would like to share with you. This system is based on numerology and astrology, and I have found it to be a source of understanding and insight about life purpose, experience, aspirations, and challenges. Each birthday (day and month) maps to one of the 52 cards of the deck. Each card has several different birthdays mapped to it. This is called the birth card, which reveals the primary purpose of an individual's life. Most birthdays have an additional card, the planetary ruling card. Planetary ruling cards indicate our personality traits in this life.

Cards of Destiny helped me discover that my life purpose is to be of service by sharing ideas and spiritual understanding while relying on my premonition and intuition. Cards of Destiny also helped me discover some of my life challenges: overcoming fear of rejection and the need to sacrifice for others in order to make choices for my own authentic happiness.

However, we are not fixed into one or two cards. Birth cards point to a collection of karma and personality traits and help us understand the expression of our personality, such as subconsciously repeating reactive patterns. Cards of Destiny helps me have compassion and understanding for myself and others, freeing me from subconscious repetition. For example, in friendships, I often fill the role of the spiritual teacher. The cards helped me see that, while standing in this role, I need to be aware of my tone, so my comments don't come across as criticism. The card's system also indicates that I should be careful not to feel criticized by my spiritual teacher. Instead, I need to remain teachable and open to learning from her.

When I was introduced to the Cards of Destiny in 2012, it was an interesting tool to understand my gifts, blind spots, and challenges. It also showed me how cards of each birthday energetically interact with each other. I find it very interesting and important to understand the dynamics of the relationship between friends and family members, and partners. For example, one friend's Cards of Destiny is the seven of clubs. Knowing this helps me understand that one of my roles in his life is to support my friend; however, I should not be surprised if he ignores my suggestions. Over several years of experimentation, I have found such information to be very accurate.

I hope this brief story of my journey to this moment, along with the Cards of Destiny system, will help you in your journey to understand yourself more deeply and to express yourself more authentically. To learn more about what I offer, visit www.shervinhojat.com

Author **Shervin Hojat** writes as a way to share the tools and techniques that have enabled him to challenge his beliefs, accept and love himself, improve his relationships, and be present and appreciative of life's simple joys. Shervin has published two other books, *Tend to Your Garden Within,* a collection of personal essays and poems published in 2008, and *Symphony of My Heart,* a poetry book published in 2019. Shervin has been writing inspiring and thought-provoking blogs since 2008. Shervin was born in Tehran, Iran, and moved to the United States to go to college. In addition to his Ph.D. in Electrical Engineering, Shervin has studied many healing and self-discovery modalities, including Reiki, Shamanism, Conscious Language, meditation, Cards of Destiny and John Maxwell coaching training. He enjoys nature, photography, poetry, writing, and dancing tango. You can visit Shervin online at www.shervinhojat.com

CHAPTER 17

ONE SIMPLE VOICE

TEACHINGS FROM A SHATTERED HEART

Joseph Uveges, Singer/Songwriter

I can recall a few times in my life; usually, after a particularly wonderful musical performance, someone would approach me and say, "Joe, that was incredible. I wish I had your life." I remember feeling sheepish at this vulnerability. I could see how I looked to them: talented singer/songwriter, good performer, lovely wife engaged in her own passionate work, two beautiful kids, a successful side career, and a small amount of fame in our geographical region. "I wish I had your life."

No one says that to me anymore.

In the early morning of May 19, 2016, I noticed that my son Andrew's bedroom door is slightly ajar, and he's not in his bed. Andrew is 11 days shy of his 16th birthday, filled with the mighty adolescent act of self-determination. He is extremely private. Something is wrong.

I peer into his room. As my head goes further in, I see his bare feet revealed behind the door. Striving to make sense of this, my first thought is Dear Lord. He's had a seizure that has shaken him out of bed and across the entire room. I enter and can immediately see in the dim light from a still running iPod that he is dead.

I kneel, trying to understand what I'm seeing. I have a sense that there is something dark behind his head. Then, to my right, I see what looks like a handgun. I touch it with a finger, not believing what I'm seeing, and the instant my finger confirms cold steel, I feel my life shatter. I hear someone start to scream. It's me.

I was raised a farm kid outside a small upstate New York town, the oldest of four boys. My parents were both of Hungarian descent and the first of their generation to go to college. Both became teachers. They were raised in working-class families (coal mining/farming), and the juxtaposition of these two ethics (hard work and education) formed the backdrop of my childhood. As is often the case with immigrant families, there was also an immense amount of pressure to perform and a certain rigidity to how life should be lived. Catholicism, with all its complexities (both beautiful and terrible), was a huge factor as well. My own parenting informed these values. Of course, there was also a beautiful simplicity to this farm life. I loved roaming the woods with my three brothers, working the farm, hunting, fishing, sports, and music. I gobbled up life, convinced it would give me all I desired.

It did. I graduated from a prestigious small college with honors, then spent some time studying to be a priest in Washington, DC. When that didn't quite resonate, my inner gypsy led me on an extended journey across Mexico and finally to Colorado, where I met my wife, Kristen. We were both in massage school, and I was drawn to her like a magnet. The feeling was mutual. We married in July of 1991.

I was working as a massage therapist, but my true passion was my budding life as a singer/songwriter. I was a trained pianist but had fallen in love with the guitar in college. I devoted myself to getting better, performing at every possible venue, working hard at the craft of songwriting, and invariably yearning for that elusive artistic achievement: fame.

The problem with fame is precisely that: it's elusive. You never really arrive at a destination that satisfies your ego. I didn't understand this at the time.

The net effect of this was excitement, anxiety, and depression. I was exhilarated and frustrated in equal measure. Each achievement was celebrated as a next step but was never enough. My life was beautiful and complete, but I couldn't see how fortunate I was.

The police and firefighters arrive. They separate me from my wife. I realize that they are assuming this is a murder scene and the only way to ascertain what has happened is by comparing our respective stories and looking for what does not fit. "Sir, why didn't you call us sooner?" "How could you not have heard the gun go off?" I am in shock. They take pictures. The coroner arrives. They place

Andrew in a black body bag, hoist his lanky frame to a gurney, and begin to wheel him out of our house for the last time.

Kristen stops them. "Please, open the bag so I can kiss him one more time."

"Ma'am, that might not be a good idea."

She insists, and they relent. The zipper is unzipped. It reveals Andrew's plastic face. She kisses him and whispers her love. I also bend over to kiss him and say something that I still find unbelievable. "Buddy. I love you. I. . .I trust you." The notion that some other aspect of me was being revealed in that instant was unfathomable. "I trust you," even now, seems a shocking leap of faith.

It's impossible to describe the devastation that follows the suicide of a child. Since there were no obvious explanations (no note, no fight), my mind searched the past for tangible causes for his choice. Over the coming months, I revisited every incident where my parenting might have been flawed. I took each interaction, replaying it repeatedly, cementing into my mind an increasingly condemnatory interpretation of our history. Even memories that were generally wonderful were revisited through the lens of this tragedy.

Who was Andrew, though? What kind of person was he? He was, in a word, fearless. An incredible physical learner, he threw himself into all physical activity with an abandon that frightened my wife and me. He was the first kid up the climbing wall, with or without protection. On an Outward-Bound trip, he climbed to the top of the zip-line pole numerous times before anyone else had the courage to do it once. He was the first kid to jump off the huge boulder 20 feet down into the Eleven Mile Canyon stream. At ten, he climbed to the very top of a 50-foot pine to rescue his cat, Jasmine.

He loved camping, shooting guns, rollerblades, his friends, mac-n-cheese, and taming untamable cats. He was an inspired wrestler. One day his coach, who we loved, watched Andrew flip a kid that was pinning him with such force that the kid literally flew off him. He turned to me with a grin and said, "I can teach him how to wrestle, but I can't teach that." He was amazing at puzzles and games that required mechanical problem-solving skills. If he was part of a team, he would see the solution too quickly for his mates. He often became bossy. He was almost always right.

Like many boys, he disliked school. He was smart enough but simply didn't care about it. In fourth grade, I can remember him spelling the word "always" three different ways in one paragraph. He hated math, and I was a jerk about constantly interjecting math problems into our daily life. I thought I was being helpful. This brings me to a memory from a month before his death: one I wish I could undo.

On Monday of that week, we spent a couple of hours working on math homework. On Thursday, I received an email from his teacher saying Andrew hadn't turned his homework in again. When I got home, I confronted him.

"Dad, I just forgot."

"Andrew. What? I mean, we did the f-cking homework. Just f-cking turn it in!" I was frustrated. He was embarrassed. After a few moments of verbal beratement, he looked at me and said, "You know, Dad, this is not going to be important for me in my life." He said it almost calmly, with an air of knowingness that stopped me.

"Well, that may be true, but for now, can you just jump through the d-mn hoops as best you can? I mean, if we do the homework, just, please, f-cking turn it in."

I replayed the awfulness of that moment a thousand times—my out-of-control anger and his subdued, prescient, almost noble response. I have begged him for forgiveness, knowing none would be forthcoming. I felt condemned to owning this and every other failed moment of my son's beautiful brief life. I expected to suffer until the end, and then, if there is an afterlife, I would do it, soul to soul in the hereafter. I dreaded and longed for this.

I did, however, experience a remarkable miracle in the first week after his death. It occurred at his viewing. My mother, Catherine Uveges, died of cancer in 1980. In the weeks before her death, there was a scent that accompanied her of roses and hazelnuts. It was unique, probably an amalgam of the get-well flowers sent by friends and the unorthodox treatment she was receiving; laetrile—a nut derived medicine.

We arrived at the funeral parlor for Andrew's private viewing. When it was my turn, I went and placed my hand on his chest, weeping quietly. I began thanking him for his life. I took a breath, and my heart stopped. My mother's scent hung in the air. I hadn't smelled it in more than 35 years. My mind refused to believe it. I knelt. Surely a scent must have been placed on his body. Nothing. It was in the air above him. *This can't be. It's impossible.* Yet, roses and hazelnuts filled the space above his body. My mother was sending me a message of consolation.

The first year after Andrew's death was agony. I'd often pray the rosary while driving to work. Sometimes I'd just whisper, "I'm sorry. I'm so sorry. Please forgive me," like a mantra of remorse. I also noticed that whenever I went to the bathroom, I would be overcome with emotion. The moment I entered the stall, I would put my head in my hands and weep. It took me more than a year to recognize PTSD. The last thing I did before my life fell apart was go to the bathroom.

My wife, Kristen, and I clung together. Our lives shrank into a tiny space: our jobs, a few friends/relatives, and each other. We saw our daughter, Katie, and her partner, Taylor, when we could. We ate alone almost every night and shared our grief openly. On a good day, we might share a dream about Andrew or an insight we felt he'd given us about how to fix some mechanical issue. "Andrew dropped in today and gave me an idea on how to repair that stove handle. Brilliant." Hearing his name was music. It still is.

At the 20-month mark, I attended a Catholic men's retreat in Divide, Colorado. Our planning team invited a local woman, a mystic named Frannie Rose, to speak about her life. Her story was compelling. At the age of 32, she became ill with an undiagnosed disease that kept her virtually bedridden for 17 years. It was an extraordinary tale of suffering, ameliorated by a surrender in her 50th year to a God that she was not sure she believed in. This surrender led, within a few weeks, to the correct doctor (and diagnosis) that returned her to some semblance of a normal life.

During the bliss that surrounded this successful medical intervention, she became aware of a loving voice. It began to teach her about herself, gently encouraging and loving her into a new life. At first, she was concerned that she was going crazy. She sought out psychological help. The psychiatrist determined that this voice was not dangerous and surmised that Frannie was having some sort of mystical experience. This confirmed her own intuition. In time, she would ask who the voice was. It responded in terms that even an agnostic Jewish woman would understand, *I Am. I always will be.*

Over the course of the next 15 years, God taught Frannie Rose a great deal. He gently directed her into new relationships and, in time, into a teaching role which included teaching others how they too may be able to access God's gentle voice. This process included a specific journaling protocol that I heard about at the retreat.

The next morning, I found an old journal that had sat on my shelf for years. I'd never journaled, but I was a prolific songwriter, so I was familiar with being directed in this way. I followed the scant directions I learned at the retreat and asked the hardest question, "God. Am I responsible for Andrew's death?" I sat and waited.

What happened then was unexpected. I heard words of tenderness. Acknowledgment. Understanding. I wrote them down. I felt the words as much as I heard them. Over the coming weeks, I kept asking questions. Not every question was answered, but many were. The answers that came gave me insights into myself and the world.

A few weeks after starting this process, I began to think I was going crazy. I was hearing/feeling such beauty. I called Frannie Rose and asked if we could meet. She was a small blonde woman of 60 or so with remarkable playful eyes and a brilliant smile. When I arrived, she asked me about my life. She then asked me to read what I was hearing from God. I felt sheepish but began. When I read the entry of a particularly evocative and beautiful journaling session, she stopped me.

"Joe, is this your voice?"

"No."

"Why?" she asked.

"Because my inner voice is filled with self-hatred. It reminds me only of how I have failed my son. Every mistake is cataloged in my mind to remind me of my awfulness. That's the voice I recognize. That is my voice." I started to sob.

Frannie sat still for a long time. Finally, she said, "Joe, there is a remarkable miracle happening here. It seems that Andrew's death has shattered who you thought you were. This "you" was mostly ego. What you have uncovered has revealed that which is most precious: God's voice inside of you. Of course, this voice is accessible to every person, but most ignore it."

"So, I'm not going crazy?"

"Well, it may feel like this at times. Your ego will fight this experience. It is frightened of mystery, yet mystery is the actuality of our lives. We are immersed in it throughout our lives. The ego, however, will dismiss miracles as mere coincidences. It will say "crazy" where the soul coaxes "mystical.""

"What of my grief?"

"Yes. What of it?

"I'm afraid that if I stop grieving, I will lose my son."

She smiled tenderly. "This is a question for God, but grief is necessary. It shows us that we have loved. He will move you slowly, precisely as He has done thus far, to where He wishes you to be. There is no need for fear. Do the work and have faith that His words are true. Be gentle with yourself."

I am now four years into this journey. My life has been transformed in ways I never could have imagined. My wife and I are in a beautiful place. I'm grateful to God/Jesus/the All for these teachings. They are further amplified by daily walks where I ask God to direct my eye toward sights that may have metaphorical meanings for me. Each visual becomes another tool of God's teaching and physical confirmation that I'm being directed.

My grief is not gone. Sorrow remains the ever-present doorway for me to re-discover my heart, so I cry regularly. It's critical. I've discovered many things on this journey: that I am not a victim of Andrew's death; that my true identity is: child of God; that rigid beliefs/opinions in any form are ego; that my mind fabricates awful stories out of the tiniest sliver of truth; that these stories are aimed at making me suffer because suffering brings me a greater sense of self; that every experience (whether I've behaved well, or poorly) is an opportunity for learning; that I am connected to and part of every other living being in the world. Possibly the most beautiful lesson is that tenderness remains the most powerful tool of my transformation.

Andrew is doing fine in his new realm. I miss him dearly. His suicide has impacted many people. It has saved some lives. It's changed me, and I'm grateful to him for everything.

I yearn to tell you of God's eternal abiding love for you:
But you will not believe me.
Your mind folding and folding in on itself with overlapping stories of
Failure and Remorse - Past projecting onto Future and back again.
But just now. For an instant. As that last breath departed
We smiled together and my mind went silent.
My son, shortly after his death imparted
"I am so grateful to be out of that mind."
Dear One. I finally understand what you meant:
God has forgiven all that my ego demanded.
It seems He can only recall my heart's longing.
This then I give to Him, and to you dear, for you
Are inside Him as well.
I wish to tell you of God's deep abiding love for you
But I see, now. You already know it. ©Uveges 2022

Joe Uveges, originally from Schoharie, New York, now lives in Colorado Springs, Colorado, with his wonderful wife of 30 years, Kristen. He is a graduate of Union College (1982) and has spent two years doing graduate work in theology at Catholic University. A professional singer/songwriter for 33 years, he's released eight studio albums. His band, The BUS Band, performs regularly on the Front Range of Colorado. He's played services for virtually every religious tradition and has found that though their congregations and belief systems may vary, there are seeds of the divine everywhere. He works closely with the non-profit that inspired this journey, One Simple Voice. This organization was originally founded by Frannie Rose and Richard Hanifen, Bishop Emeritus of the Diocese of Colorado Springs. (onesimplevoice.org) Joe and Kristen recently celebrated the birth of their first grandchild, a boy, born to their daughter Katie (a musician as well) and her partner, Taylor. You can find him at Joe Uveges Musician (Facebook), Joseph Uveges (Signal), josephuveges (Instagram), and jkuveges@pcisys.net

CHAPTER 18

FROM DRUG ADDICT TO SOUND HEALER

A JOURNEY OF TRANSFORMATION

Kelvin Young

I spent a life addicted to alcohol and other drugs and then eventually became a certified sound healer. My life had its difficulties. I struggled with cocaine, heroin, marijuana, prescription opioids, and alcohol. Like many of us, I had some emotional and mental health issues. But I tried to solve my problems by using alcohol and other drugs. These addictions brought with them immense depression and anxiety. I dealt with drug addiction, depression, and anxiety for years.

I spent a life not worth living before recovery. I felt emotionally bankrupt. The years of letting myself and others down, the horrible crimes I committed, and the physical pain I've caused to the people who loved me the most took a heavy toll on my heart. I have a few happy memories from that period of my life. I got involved in stealing, robbing people, selling drugs, and living a very fast criminal lifestyle. I never had a healthy romantic relationship; I was physically and verbally abusive. I was involved in a few automobile accidents and have been arrested for driving under the influence of alcohol and other drugs. I spent over 20 years fighting addictions, but you would be here all day if I started telling you every story of hardship. Going to prison changed my life forever. I was sentenced to five years and suspended after 26 months with four-year probation.

I call that time a blessing in disguise and divine intervention. It was as if the Universe intervened. I was taken out of my comfort zone, a life of addiction, and put into prison, where I had the opportunity to change my life. A few programs are provided to incarcerated men and women willing to make a positive change in themselves. The most helpful program for me was the Tier Three Drug Treatment Program. That program taught me how the drugs I took affected me and how my mind and body were under the direct influence because of these drugs. I learned about substance use disorder and holistic modalities to heal myself.

My life-changing practice was meditation. I remember sitting in the lotus position with other inmates and having so many thoughts in my head. I heard the snickering from other inmates because we were practicing meditation. But I closed my eyes and focused on the calming words from the meditation instructor who was serving a 20-year prison sentence. When I started to meditate, I was able to find peace with myself. I felt a sense of calmness even being in a very hostile and restrictive environment such as prison. With the programs, I was able to find out how to help myself become a better person. My beautiful daughter Tatiyana motivated me to change myself and become what I am today. When she came to visit me, I was still able to see the twinkle in my daughter's eye for her dad. She wanted to tell me everything that was going on in her life. She inspired me to become the man she wanted as her father, a man she could look up to. That's what I needed to change my destiny; a daughter's love for her father.

When I look back, I find the root causes of my problems were in my childhood. I was kept back in kindergarten. I didn't feel good enough. I dealt with a lot of self-esteem, self-hatred, and self-worth issues. I endured emotional trauma, which caused me emotional pain throughout my adolescent, teenage, and adult years. I started using drugs and alcohol to cope with it; they gave me relief. The escape I found in these substances helped me overcome the chronic stress in my mind and body. My stress used to get temporarily relieved from alcohol, cocaine, marijuana, heroin, and prescription opioids. There was not only stress but also intense sadness and feelings of anxiety. But there were always negative emotions and consequences.

Meditation is collectively a set of practices that encourage focused attention and a heightened state of awareness. It is a consciousness-changing technique, and it has been proven to help a person's psychological well-being. There are two basic types of meditation:

- Concentrative meditation includes zeroing in your consideration on something particular while blocking out all the other things around you. To arrive at a higher condition, the objective is to encounter anything you are zero in on, whether your breath, a particular word, sound, or a mantra.

- Mindfulness meditation incorporates, among others, both Mindfulness-based Stress Reduction (MBSR) and Mindfulness-based Cognitive Therapy (MBCT). Care and mindfulness can target various issues, such as sorrow, implying that its center might be unique from practice to rehearsing. Generally speaking, it includes the condition of monitoring and engaging with the current second and making yourself open, mindful, and in the present moment.

POSITIVE EFFECTS OF MEDITATION

Consciousness is frequently compared to a stream, moving and changing flawlessly as it disregards the territory. Meditation is one purposeful method for steering this stream and, thus, changing how you see and answer your general surroundings. Research has demonstrated how meditation can make both physiological and mental impacts. A portion of the positive physiological effects incorporate a brought down condition of actual excitement, diminished breath rate, diminished pulse, changes in brainwave patterns, and brought down stress.

A few of the other mental, profound, and well-being related advantages of meditation include:

- Better administration of side effects connected with nervousness problems, gloom, rest issues, torment issues, and hypertension

- Better pressure on the executive abilities

- Changes in various parts of consideration and care

- Expanded self-awareness

- Further developed close to home prosperity

- Worked on working memory and fluid intelligence

- Further developed insusceptibility
- More noteworthy compassion for you and others
- Migraine help

Meditation changed my life. Inside the prison, I started taking the programs of meditation, yoga, and sound healing. I became self-aware and a better person due to these holistic modalities. I started practicing expressive arts, like journaling and poetry. Before beginning the practice of meditation and other holistic practices, I had a lot of misconceptions about them. I used to think meditation was only practiced by Buddhists and hippies and that yoga was only for wealthy, privileged white women because that is how yoga is marketed in the United States. As a Black man, a person of color, I didn't think these holistic practices were for me. Therefore, I never even tried to implement them.

Adopting that mindset was the best thing that happened to me. I changed how I lived my life. I was heading to an early grave with the way I was living. My way of life before divine intervention was out of control. I had a pessimistic attitude, a huge chip on my shoulder. The reckless way I drove, the numerous fights I got into, and the altercation with the police were direct reflections of that.

I was not able to see the vicious cycle I was stuck in. I'd have kept going on in the same addicted lifestyle if it was not for counseling, my supportive family, and sober friends. They showed me the right path in life. These holistic practices allowed me to see things differently. I have learned how to creatively express the emotions I've suppressed for many years under alcohol and other drugs through journaling and poetry. Meditating with sound allowed me to go within, see and feel all my feelings—the shame and guilt—the things that often keep people like myself in that vicious cycle of addiction.

I moved past the shame and guilt and realized my true essence as a spiritual human being. I realized that the true nature of humanity is **unconditional, agape love.** The deeper I learned about the healing power of sound, the more I realized that love is more than human emotion. I understand that love is a vibration, a frequency, and our natural state of being. Often our past traumas, social conditions, culture, and programming make us feel disconnected from this inner love that dwells in all of us. Sound healing and meditation connected me back to this truth.

I believe healing is about understanding our wholeness. We're more than our physical bodies. We have mental, emotional, and *spiritual* aspects that make up the totality of who we truly are. Life does not have any meaning until we look into ourselves. Most of the people in our modern-day society do not even know their true potential, and some just spend their lives like robots. People live with their traumas without even trying to heal and recover. Healing with practices like sound healing, meditation, and yoga shift our states of consciousness. I shifted the way I see myself, the world, and the people in it. Sound healing literally transformed my life!

Once I was released from prison, I dove deep into sound healing and went to get certified in the practice that saved my life. I'm extremely passionate about introducing as many people as I can to the transformative power of sound. My intention is to make sound healing mainstream within our culture that deals with so many challenges both individually and collectively. Being experienced myself, I know how many people can be helped with the healing power of sound, and my intention is to offer sound healing to as many people as possible.

Today, I'm a certified Sound Healer and a Recovery Support Specialist. I facilitate sound healing sessions for people from different walks of life. I provide peer support to people to help overcome mental health, addiction, and trauma-related issues. I understand people. I know many others face problems I once faced. I was an addict, a thief, a criminal, and an unhealthy person. I helped myself out of the situation, and now I help others get out of their hell hole. I provide sound healing and peer recovery coaching sessions to help transform their lives to work best for them. I am a person who has not used alcohol or any other drug since March 6, 2009. I have been sober and haven't used any sort of substance to cope with my emotional issues. I'm a survivor. Human beings are very resilient. Now, I help others recover from their addiction issues through sound healing.

I would like to end by sharing a poem I wrote while in prison after practicing meditation with sound, which was the catalyst for my transformation. Even if this poem and chapter help a single person, my purpose is done.

Eyes of a Silent Son

Look into my eyes and tell me what you see.
Is it a lost soul with no control trying to be free?
As I look into the mirror and stare into my eyes,
I see all the anger and self-hate, hypocrisy and lies.
I see resentment, frustration, embarrassment, and pain,
I see jail bars and fancy cars as I cruise down memory lane.
I see the feelings I repressed, going back to childhood.
I need to let go of all those feelings, and I would if I could.
I see the hurt I caused to the ones I love the most.
I see my brother on his wedding day as we celebrate with a toast.
I see the good and the bad times that I experienced in my life.
But it's so hard to let go of all that bitterness and strife.
There's a sense of sadness when you look into my eyes.
Like the ones, you see when a close relative dies.
But this death is not physical; it has to do with the soul.
It's that morbid feeling we get when our spiritual energy is low.
It's like nothing matters anymore, like that day when I was fired,
Feeling depressed and weak can't sleep, but I'm so tired.
I'm tired of all the pain, the hurt, and the rain.
From that cloud that keeps following me, sometimes I think I'm insane.
But when I look out my window and see the beauty of the lake.
It reminds me of good times, like when I was nine, and things were fine.
And with the sunrise, I feel the presence of the Creator.
When I look out my window, I see myself in the beauty of nature.
I'm a part of God's creation, nature, and humanity!
The loving spirit that's in Jesus is also in me!
So I've learned to love myself and others just for who we are.
And I learned about this love looking out my window with jail bars.

Kelvin Young is a certified Sound Healer and owner of Kelvin Young, LLC. He is also a person in sustained recovery, which means Kelvin hasn't used alcohol or any other drug to cope with his mental and emotional distress since March 6, 2009. Kelvin received his Recovery Support Specialist (RSS) certification at Recovery University. (Advocacy Unlimited) and his recovery coaching training at CT Community for Addiction Recovery. (CCAR) He is also trained in Intentional Peer Support (IPS) and Emotional CPR. (eCPR)

Kelvin has presented around the country in diverse settings, including yoga studios, retreat centers, conferences, schools, colleges, prisons, treatment centers, psychiatric hospitals, and mental health agencies. He also was presented with the 2017 Dr. F. Marcus Brown Memorial Integrative Medicine Award for exceptional commitment to incorporating integrative medicine within CT Valley Hospital, a state psychiatric hospital. He also received the 2021 Deron Drumm Excellence in Integrative Medicine Award from the CT Statewide Behavioral Health Integrative Medicine Collaborative.

Kelvin is the co-founder of Toivo, a peer-run holistic healing center in Hartford, CT. He was also inducted into the CT Hall of Change in September 2020, designed to recognize formerly incarcerated men and women who have made substantial contributions to CT communities since their release. Kelvin was also featured in a powerful documentary on trauma, addiction, and recovery called {Uprooting Addiction.}

Kelvin sustains his recovery by eating a vegetarian diet, practicing sound healing, deep breathing exercises, listening to uplifting and relaxing music, body movement, being in nature, reading, massages, resting, and connecting with loved ones. Today, Kelvin facilitates sound healing sessions and publicity speaks on addiction recovery at different locations throughout the United States. He is passionate about holding space for people to heal and is known for his warm, loving, and down-to-earth way of connecting with people. Contact Kelvin at: www.kelvinbyoung.com

CHAPTER 19

CYCLING TO A NEW YOU

DISCOVERING WHO YOU ARE
ONE MILE AT A TIME

Scott Bell, Certified Transformational Coach

I always thought I knew what it meant to be me. I tried to be good and do the right thing all my life. I always told myself: *I am a good person,* which was good enough for me. I had a sense of being good and right in who I was. Those feelings led to my behavior in life and my daily actions.

Throughout most of my adult life, I never knew I was not being myself but rather being the person I thought others needed me to be or how I felt I should be to fit in and measure up to those around me. I always thought *I just wanted to fit in,* wherever I was, which meant bending who I was to fit the situation at the time. Everything seemed to be okay in life. I had an average military career, and during that time, I married and became a good husband and good father. Sure, like everyone, I had problems with marriage and raising children; however, I told myself *you're a good person in the grand scheme of things. You're doing what's needed to support the family.*

What I didn't know was all the people-pleasing and making sure I did the right thing was what was keeping me from being my true self. Depression and resentment built over the years. I never really knew what was causing it or why I was so depressed most of the time.

These cycles of depression would come and go. Over time, however, the depression would come more frequently, and the durations kept getting longer and longer. My wife at the time would call them my spirals. These became more and more regular. Over time, I spent more time in the deepest parts of my spiral, the abyss. After a time, the abyss became my normal state.

The spirals built momentum as one issue became another more significant issue. Thoughts like, *you are such a failure,* and *you can't do anything right,* would repeat over and over, progressively getting harsher. It only took a minor setback to trigger the spiral, and once it got going, it was like a freight train building more and more speed. There was no stopping it. Every little unfinished thing added to the weight of the train. Thoughts like, *I didn't take out the trash as I should,* lead to *I'm such a failure. Why does everything I do end up so badly?* This building of negative thought would twist my view into: *you never take the trash out on time.*

This constant self-deprecation and low self-worth would take me deeper each time I entered my spiral. On the outside, all was well, like a duck on the water. My now ex-wife knew what was happening under the water, but no one else really had any idea I was so depressed and down on myself most of the time.

I went through life like nothing was wrong. I thought I was *a good husband and father.* I would tell myself that if we didn't fight, everything must be well in my marriage. I was a master at avoidance and skirting around issues.

Over time, we started finding things to do away from each other. *Giving space is a good thing. I'm such a nice guy, and I have no issues with her going out with her girlfriends. That way, she gets what she needs, and I can go hang out with my friends and get what I need.* These were some of the most flawed thoughts I had. I was having fun with my friends and she with hers. What we believed we were doing was giving each other needed space. Instead, we grew apart. We were avoiding our issues.

Shortly after returning from a year-long deployment as a contractor in Afghanistan, I got the news. It was the Friday before our 22nd wedding anniversary, and we each made plans to go out with our respective friends. Our understanding was that we would be home reasonably early to kick off our anniversary festivities at home. I got home early and thought, *I just don't want to do anything tonight. Something is wrong, off somehow.* In reality, something had been off since I returned from the deployment. I got ready for bed and pretended to be asleep when she got home.

Saturday morning started like usual. Nothing out of the ordinary. I stayed in bed to wait and see if we could kindle a bit of a spark since nothing had happened the night before. While she was at the sink, I told her about my dream Friday night.

> "We're in a big house, almost what could be called a mansion. The kids were no longer living there, and we were the only ones living in the house. You were packing your clothes to move to another room at the other end of the house. Why are you going to move to another room? So far away. I don't understand."

As I finished telling my wife about the dream, I couldn't believe the look on her face. There was worry and sadness. Still clueless, I couldn't for the life of me understand what was going on. That's when I got the news. *I never saw it coming.* After knowing each other for 28 years, it all came crashing down around me. I found out that she wanted to move out of our house to find herself. Only for a short while. Nothing permanent. Only for a few months to get a chance to be on her own without the kids or me and get to know herself.

I was heartbroken. The tears would not stop. There were no sparks that morning or ever since. A few months turned into more, then to finality, divorce. She asked that we get a divorce. *Holy shit, really, after all this time?* A few months later, we filed for divorce.

Lost and broken, I had no idea what I would do with my life. At first, I thought, *Maybe this could be fun. I get to do anything I want. I don't have to ask for permission to do anything—no coordinating schedules with anyone.* I was desperately looking for a way to avoid the pain and avoid the fact that I was yet again a massive failure by my marriage ending in divorce. The depression spirals worsened. *Nothing in my life is going right.* All I could do was go to work, come home and take care of my teenager.

What was unexpected is that I started to find myself, bit by bit, over the months and years after the divorce. Once my youngest was out of the house, being on my own gave me freedom—a chance to live life on my terms. I didn't have to pretend to be the perfect husband or father. It was just me. Freedom opened the door to look deep into myself. I was able to decide who I wanted to become.

Even sometime before the divorce, I knew I didn't want to be the old me anymore. *There is a better me out there somewhere,* is what I told myself anyway. Even if, at the time, I didn't believe it myself. I started to dabble in some self-improvement videos I found. After watching for many hours, none of it seemed to be making any difference. Lots of concepts, ideas, and excellent knowledge, yet still, I wasn't doing anything to integrate the concepts I heard and read.

A short time after the divorce is when the search for myself started. I studied more. Yet, still, nothing was getting through. I didn't see any meaningful change. I could feel this deep knowing that I wanted more, anything but my life. I still had no idea where to find it or how to bring it into existence.

The days turned into weeks, then months. I knew something had to change. I looked for anything I could grasp to show me who I could be. In this grasping is when I had this crazy idea. *I'm going to do it. I'm going to ride my bicycle across the United States. Why not? After all, my former in-laws did it together, so why can't I?* Seeing what others accomplished, my unreachable dream could now be achievable.

As time passed, I started to cultivate that dream. Little by little, thoughts of the ride moved their way from some distant, unreachable goal to something attainable. The thoughts grew, and before I knew it, the idea also grew. The initial idea went from a transcontinental ride to a ride around the country's entire perimeter.

How crazy is this? I thought this many times. There was no way I could afford to take a year off of work to ride around the country. Even though I kept replaying that over and over in my head, my heart had other ideas. The desire grew, and the ride was about to happen before I knew it.

I quit my job, which I hated. It was sucking the life right out of me; *no loss there.* I sold my house and also conducted my own estate sale. I also sold my vehicles. With most of my possessions sold, I felt lighter with newfound freedom. The day I closed the sale of my home, I rented a car, loaded my bike onto a trunk rack, and set off for Seaside, Oregon.

Everything moved along with ease in planning the ride and the start of the drive west. However, that wasn't going to last more than a day. I drove west along Interstate 70 in Colorado toward Utah the following day.

I wasn't even four miles into Utah when my bicycle decided to commit suicide. The bike departed the rack on the back of the car, right on the highway.

All I could see in my rearview mirror were bike parts bouncing in all directions across both lanes of the highway. Fortunately, I was parallel to an on-ramp, so I could slam on the brakes and stop on the wide shoulder between where the on-ramp merges with the interstate. The next happy thing was there was no traffic behind me. I was able to run back and pick up the bike and the few parts I could see before anyone else passed. The bicycle didn't hit anyone, nor was it run over. The dead metal just lay on the road.

At this point, my old self would have just given up. The bike I had long trained on, had so meticulously tuned and tweaked for the ride, was now in shambles. But something was different. I was not angry or sad at all. I put the battered bicycle back on the rack and proceeded west. I stopped and camped with some old friends from my Hill Air Force days. I went to Ogden to find a bike shop the next morning. The shop was unable to fix my bike at that time. However, they gave me a great recommendation for a shop in Portland, Oregon. River City Bicycles was able to set me up with a whole new bike. They let me use a workstation to swap what was salvageable off the old bike and install what I needed on the new one. Although untested, my new Surly Long Haul Trucker was ready to go a few hours later. I proceeded from there to Seaside, where the adventure was to begin.

As the ride progressed, so did the trust in myself. Little did I know the profound changes I would experience on the ride. My most notable changes were going from rarely finishing anything of importance to completing this ride of over 12,000 miles in a little less than seven months of riding time. The other is the ease at which the whole trip happened. Everything was easy, from planning the ride, getting up each morning, packing the bike, and getting back on the saddle.

As I spent time riding long empty roads, it gave me time to think. Mostly time to heal. I learned ways to clear my head and forgive others like my ex-wife. Mostly I learned to forgive myself. I still didn't fully understand how and why the ride happened so effortlessly until much later, after the ride was over. I realized it wasn't who I wanted to become but who I was at the time. I learned that I became the person who already rode around the perimeter even before I started the trip. I found this to be the key to change. Change isn't about willpower or forcing yourself to achieve a goal. It's about genuinely embodying who the person is that you want to become.

In hindsight, I see how my narrative changed in the months before the ride. I went from thinking, *I want to do a transcontinental ride,* evolving to, *I'm going to ride my bike across the country,* and eventually thinking, *I am riding my bike around the perimeter of the United States.* There are subtle differences between these thoughts. I went from having a want to having a goal. It changed further to the embodiment of someone riding, or who has already ridden, around the perimeter.

It may not seem like a difference as the narrative changed, but it is. The ease at which I could plan and execute the ride came with the belief, no actually, it came with a knowingness, that I was someone who had already accomplished the ride. As a result, when it came time to sit in the saddle and do the ride, it wasn't something I had to overcome and achieve because I already embodied the person who accomplished that ride.

Finding the ease in accomplishing goals is the basis of everything I work on for myself. I want to share what I learned the hard way and teach others how to find clarity and perspective without having the same heartache and trauma. I found this to be the key to achieving results for myself and my clients.

When we change our perspective and embody the emotion of what it's like to have that outcome already, then we become a person that is grateful and connected to that outcome. Once that happens, our actions line up with our goal, and we become the person who achieves any result that we desire with ease.

I work every day on changing how I feel. I start with connecting to gratitude. I have gratitude for everything I have and, more importantly, everything I want. I help others to change their perspectives. One way that I accomplish this is by being in the saddle. Riding for me is my meditation, my release, and a way to clear negative thoughts and energy out of my mind and body.

I work on awareness of myself in the reality that I know. Once we identify those patterns and feelings, we gain knowledge. We can then use that knowledge to change ourselves. For me, being in the saddle is a tool to connect to desire, reprogram ourselves, and transcend who we currently are to someone beyond our wildest dreams. I like to say that I'm changing one mile at a time.

Scott Bell is a certified Transformational Life Coach and workshop leader for people looking for lasting change. He works with individuals who know they want to change but haven't been able to attain it. His unique style of using cycling, along with his one-to-one coaching, brings deep and lasting results.

Scott also partners with his soul mate Kelly leading a program called Connected Love for couples. Working with couples to give them the tools they need to problem solve any relationship challenge. As we know, conflict is a natural part of life and is inevitable in relationships. They help couples learn skills to take the stress and anxiety out of conflict to enjoy the connection and love they are seeking.

Scott is retired Air Force, where he worked in several career fields. From technical areas like Precision Measurement Equipment Laboratory Technician (electronic calibration and repair), Technical Controller (telecommunications and networking), and then retiring as a Chaplain's Assistant. His unique experience and combination of skills give him unmatched insight into problems. He is able to pull issues apart and get to the root of the problem.

He is a passionate cyclist. He loves long-distance cycling. His volunteer efforts with Adaptive Adventures help bring miles of smiles.

If you want to change your life one mile at a time and are interested in working with Scott, please contact him:

For individual coaching www.transformationcycling.com

For couples www.connectedlove.us

Scott@transformationcycling.com

CHAPTER 20

I DON'T KNOW HOW TO LIVE

LIFE IS A JOURNEY, NOT A DESTINATION

Gene Wright, RYT® 500, Certified Recovery Coach

As I stared from the back of the ambulance at the dark-colored SUV, which always seemed to show up when I was using cocaine, a voice from deep inside came like thunder, *I don't know how to live.* This was very different from all the times before, desperate moments when I'd make a promise to something beyond me. *Help me this time, and I swear I won't do that again!*

Growing up in a household filled with alcoholism and co-dependence was emotionally confusing, and when my parents divorced, I stopped believing in anything, especially in a loving God. We moved from a suburban Southern California home to a trailer park in Fresno. I began using alcohol and drugs to mask the pain and rage in me.

My first drug experience happened while walking along the beach with friends when one of them handed me a joint. I remember taking that first hit and it moving through my body. I immediately felt a sense of peace I hadn't yet experienced in my life. My mind stopped spinning, and the pain and anger were gone. This was a fantastic feeling I would chase throughout my life.

I abused alcohol and drugs for the next decade to escape every good or bad feeling. I just did not want to feel anything. Cocaine found me through my sister's boyfriend. We were going to a Supertramp concert that evening, and he asked if I would like a snort, and I said, "Of course, I would." Three seconds after I snorted the white powder, I was rocketed into a state of euphoria. The concert started, and it was just Supertramp and me, and nothing else mattered. The lights were brighter, the sounds were mesmerizing, and my mind and body were one.

I entered military service when I was 19 in an attempt to quit using. That proved ineffective, as the urge to drink and use drugs was too strong. I was in pain, angry, and alone. I was discharged after three and a half years because of cocaine use.

I called in sick off base after spending three days snorting cocaine. I couldn't speak that day, and my body was completely numb. The shower water did not even register on my body. I stumbled into the office and was immediately escorted to the base hospital for a urine test. As my manager walked with me after the test was complete, he asked me, "How much cocaine did you use?" I did not say anything because I did not want to admit to using, and I did not want to lie if the test returned positive. After a pause, he joked, "Your urine was so saturated with cocaine that the lab techs were getting high!"

In 1986, my family and friends staged an intervention. I went into a 28-day twelve-step hospital treatment program, and I was able to stay dry for 13 years. During that time, I held a steady job, got married, bought a house, and looked like I enjoyed being normal. Halfway through the marriage, I began to feel restless, irritable, and discontent with my life. I did not use anything, but I did have an affair. This was a form of addictive behavior because I was not taking care of the underlying issues causing my addiction.

The marriage ended in divorce, and I was laid off from the job I had for eleven years. I started taking prescription pain pills and illegal narcotics. For the next four years, I went through the darkest moments of my life up to that point in time. I was admitted to a psych ward because I was a danger to myself and others.

The first time I was admitted, the police came, and I was afraid and confused. They were somewhat friendly as they put me into handcuffs. Later, restrained in a straight jacket, I thought, *I've really done it this time.* As I sat alone in the rubber room, I thought, *I need to get out of here.* So,

I dislocated my left shoulder, took off the jacket, and ran out of the room down the hallway with the attendants chasing me.

The exit doors were in front of me, and so was freedom. I went through the doors, and the security officer standing there asked me, "Where are you going?"

I said, "Out of here." He laughed and asked me to look and see how I was dressed. That's when I realized I didn't have any clothes on. They marched me back into the rubber room, put the straight-jacket on so tight I could hardly breathe, and strapped it to the table. After a few days, I was released and went back out into the world, still feeling the same pain, anger, and loneliness.

Two weeks later, I was back in the psych ward after chasing a woman in my apartment complex, thinking she was out to get me. The same police officers came to my door. They were again kind and asked if I would like to take a few days to get better, and I agreed. After several days, I was asked if I wanted to be admitted to another twelve-step hospital treatment program, which I accepted. I was able to stay dry for another four years before I started using drugs and alcohol again.

I dealt with alcohol blackouts and abused prescription pain pills and cocaine during this time. In the summer of 2015, I found myself in the back of that ambulance in another blackout, having shot up three and a half grams of cocaine. That day started like any other day: pain pills to mend the pain and hangover from the day before, double Baileys and coffee to wake up, and a six-pack of beer to get ready to play golf.

I was tired of living that way, and my overdose was a cry for help. Later, a therapist would tell me, "There are other ways of asking for help." Friends of mine found Summit Estate while I was sitting on the bench outside the hospital the next day, and they encouraged me to give it a try. I did not want to go to another twelve-step hospital treatment program.

Summit Estate's approach to recovery was different—a holistic view of overall health. There, I learned healthy ways to deal with my addiction and how to live differently, without drugs and alcohol.

They taught me how to sit with myself, breathe when confronted with difficult situations, eat and hydrate, meditate, and even start practicing yoga—simple steps that worked. I would walk around the grounds, stop at the pond, watch the ducks, and dream of a simple life.

Summit Estate introduced me to this holistic approach to recovery, which is different from the twelve-step hospital treatment program. They taught me to take care of all the aspects of life to gain proper healing. I stayed for the recommended 40 days and continued with the intensive outpatient eight-week program to further understand myself. My body and mind were starting to feel better, and I had a sense of hope. After the outpatient program, I entered an eight-week recovery coaching program that continued my progress.

During the eight-week program, I met Tommy Rosen, the founder of Recovery 2.0, while vacationing in Jamaica. We played a round of golf. I was playing the club's golf pro for money. After hitting my opening tee shot into the row of trees a hundred yards to the left, he asked me, "Have you ever had a mental lesson?" As we talked, walking to my ball, he said, "You prepare for everything you have control over, and once you start the swing, you have to let go of all expectations."

The shot called for the ball to go under a branch, rise to miss trees ahead, and hook about 50 yards. After imaging the shot, I swung the club and let go of the result. I did not even see where the ball went and started talking to Tommy right after the shot, asking, "What's the next lesson?"

The ball landed on the green about five yards away from the hole, and after making the putt, I was 1-up on the golf pro playing alongside us. I do not remember much about the match, but that pro did owe me a few dollars by the end.

Walking the course with Tommy, I discovered that the universe supported me. He told me, "Feel how the ground supports you as you walk, how gravity keeps you from floating into space." He pointed out that all the green that I saw was breathing in what I was breathing out, and I was breathing in what they were breathing out. I had learned that in school somewhere, but until that moment, it didn't click. Standing there on that golf course, surrounded by green, I felt connected to the universe for the first time in my life.

Soon after, I was introduced to the practice of Kundalini yoga, which taught me how to move energy throughout my body and gave me the high

I looked for in drugs and alcohol. I realized I didn't need to look outside myself to find comfort in a substance. Soon, I was doing Kundalini yoga and meditation with 2000 people at a yoga retreat and finding inner peace. At that point, I knew I wanted to devote my life to understanding and sharing yoga, so I started my yoga teacher training, which continues through today.

Meanwhile, I started the process of the twelve steps with a teacher who took me on a year-long journey through the program. Thanks to this work, I had a spiritual awakening, as described in step twelve. The first three steps built the foundation; steps four through nine helped me take a deep dive, and my spiritual maintenance was in steps ten and eleven and assisting others in step twelve.

After I completed the twelve steps, I started to have intimate relationships, which brought me back to all the underlying causes and conditions of my addiction: co-dependence. Soon, I found a bottom I hadn't experienced before, and it didn't involve a substance but rather a deep grieving of all the losses and hurts I'd suffered and all the pain I caused in my life. It was so painful I wanted to end this life of despair and pain and move on to the next.

Because the urge to use drugs and alcohol was removed by the spiritual awakening, they were no longer an option for me. I spent many days and nights in a fetal position crying tears of grief and feeling immense pain within my body. A teacher suggested I take time to find out who Gene is all about. They told me to become my own soulmate, which I was looking for.

I worked on the twelve steps of co-dependence, which gave me a new understanding. I studied Richard Rohr's, *Breathing Under Water,* which gave me hope. I read and meditated using Pema Chodron's book *When Things Fall Apart: Heart Advice for Difficult Times* in order not to escape the pain and suffering.

After a year, I found myself at a retreat with Dr. Joe Dispenza, opening my heart in a way that is hard to describe. I continued to take my yoga teacher training courses, read books, listen to podcasts, and study the practices of the shamans. I discovered threads of truth running through all these teachings that linked them together as one.

Then, I discovered plant medicine and participated in ceremonies that helped me navigate emotional, sexual, and physical trauma from childhood.

The plant medicine brought light into the darkest and scariest parts of me to bring back those fragmented pieces and restore me to a sense of wholeness. This type of treatment is sometimes looked down upon in the recovery community, but I knew these ceremonies were necessary for my recovery.

For me, the most crucial experience in plant medicine was the revelation that the things that happened when I was very young were not my fault. I could now forgive those who hurt me and understand that they were spiritually sick, just like I was. I could forgive myself for all the physical, mental, emotional, sexual, and spiritual abuse I had brought upon myself.

This forgiveness gave me the understanding that what happened was *for* me and my evolution in order to learn how to let go of my story of myself as a victim. Life can happen to you, for you, or through you. I now choose to have life happen through me and to live with an open heart. I'm here to trust, gain wisdom, balance my energy, and achieve abundance and prosperity.

Tommy Rosen once told me, "The Universe has considered your story." I now genuinely believe it has. These past years, I have embarked upon many paths as I discover who I am: a human being having a spiritual experience, using all of my senses.

Somewhere along the way, I was given the medicine name Gene Keeps the Way, and I fully embrace this new identity. I believe that there are many paths along the way in this journey called life.

Gene Wright, RYT® 500, Certified Recovery Coach, is the owner of Gene Wright Wellness, where his mission is living a life aligned with his Higher Self, going beyond limitations, respecting boundaries, and being reliable to himself and others with an open heart, integrity, non-judgment, and generosity.

What drew him to recovery coaching was his transformation in the mirror. He wants to help people transform so they love what they see. As a Yoga-inspired Recovery coach, twelve-Step Recovery practitioner, and Radiant Body Hatha yoga teacher, he takes a holistic approach to recovery and is committed to sharing his experience, strength, and hope with the recovery community.

When Gene chills out, you will find him with his golf clubs on a beautiful golf course or a beach in Costa Rica with something made of dark chocolate in his mouth. Joy is the way he healed himself.

Connect with Gene:

On his website: https://GeneWrightWellness.com

On Facebook: https://www.facebook.com/genewrightwellness

On Instagram: https://www.instagram.com/genewrightwellness/

CHAPTER 21

THERE IS NO SUCH THING AS A HEALTHY EGO

STEP OUT OF THE ILLUSION AND WAKE UP!

Patrick Dague

I'm sitting on a large log on an empty Southern Oregon beach as I dictate this paragraph into my phone. The morning light is rising, and I have a view of sand, rocks, and the ocean. There are a few seagulls wheeling above, and an osprey is flapping off with a small fish held in talons purpose-built to prevent the loss of its slippery breakfast. I can see from here the stairs leading up to the large clifftop home my wife and I own. It's situated on an acre-sized property well above the beach; we use it occasionally to host spiritual retreats. And what started out as a pamphlet for our retreats is now expanding into a chapter for this book. The timing feels right.

I'm an ordinary person who is enlightened. There seems to be some kind of unwritten rule against stating a truth like that right up front; some leading up to it is much more the norm when, and if, an enlightened person speaks about their own spiritual awakening. Here it is, however.

I am one of the still small but growing numbers of people in our world who've awakened to the truth of being. The result is that I no longer have an ego I identify as me. The freedom in that is enormous, and the life changes that have resulted are extraordinarily beautiful and amazing.

There is more to this story, but the short version is that I stumbled into enlightenment almost by accident when, after decades of hard work as a real estate broker and investor, I lost everything. That happened during and after the 2007 - 2009 financial crisis that crashed real estate markets all over the world. The losses I'm talking about took several years thereafter to unfold. They included my marriage, 14 rental properties (I had far too much real estate debt), my new car, almost all of my cash and liquid capital, and my home. Partners who had invested with me also lost money.

I'm a pilot and flight instructor; teaching flying is a professional hobby I enjoy. Prior to all that, I had to sell a new airplane I bought because of other past mistakes that put me in a situation where I could no longer afford it. There had been other issues in my past as well, all of which were related to my ongoing intention to create a glittering future for myself by using aggressive business strategies, leveraging debt, developing a base of cash investors, and acquiring properties. To me, the future was what mattered; whatever was happening now was always a means to an end that was to come later.

One thing I did not realize until after I lost everything was that the manager who was running my life up to that point was my ego. With it in charge, I was always reaching for something more when what I really needed was a solid foundation in the present, including a conservative and balanced financial situation. I was, in other words, like the foolish man in the Bible (Matthew 7:24-27) who built his house on sand, and when the storms came, it fell with a great crash.

There were many successes during the decades my ego was in charge, but nothing ever seemed to stick; nothing ever worked out well in the long run, no matter how hard I tried. And I did try. Then when failures happened, I tried again, and again, and again. However, with my ego as manager, the "later" I created was not what I wanted and expected. In fact, after losing everything, I was actually homeless for a while, sleeping outside.

After I lost my house, I got a job pulling gliders into the air with an old crop duster airplane at a nearby glider airport. I was paid ten dollars for each tow-flight. That was enough to buy food and a 30-year-old car. It was also fun, and the owner of the glider airport allowed me to sleep on the deck outside of the airport office. I worked there for quite a while, towing gliders up a mile or so, and I spent a lot of time between flights talking to excited customers who were next in line for a glider flight. Almost all of them seemed to be happy and at peace. I realized, to the core of my being, that what I really wanted to feel within myself was the same peace, relaxation, and the easy joy I saw in them.

One key point here is that perhaps for the first time in my life, I was focused on being entirely present in the moment. I was a low-paid tow plane pilot without a girlfriend, but I was doing something I loved, so I decided to let the future unfold by itself and do my best in the situation I was in. I eventually found a room to rent in a house not far from the glider airport, then a house to rent with a friend. After that, I slowly started back into real estate investment activities and dating.

One thing I did *not* do was make excuses for myself. My losses were all the result of decisions I alone had made, and I realized there was no point in looking outside of myself for the problem; I was the problem.

My only question, after decades of work, came crashing down like a house of cards as I found myself homeless was: what exactly needed to change in me, so I never made the same mistakes again? The easy initial answers were that I needed to start again, work hard, and be more fiscally conservative. I also realized I needed to educate myself. And that is another key point.

When I re-launched my real estate career, I decided to focus on just one area, which was finding, fixing up, and selling distressed residential properties for a profit. And this time, I made it a point to get advice from a number of real estate investment coaches, as opposed to thinking I already knew it all after several decades as an active real estate broker and investor. My interviews and discussions with those coaches eventually turned into a book titled *Real Estate Investment Coach Secrets,* which is available on Amazon.com.

During all that time, I kept my job as a tow-plane pilot, eventually working part-time instead of full time, and I kept looking within because I knew intuitively that there was something deeper and more compelling than making money or getting into another relationship. However, I did not know what I was missing. I simply knew there was something in me that was still not quite right.

I had earned significant profits in the past by buying fixer properties and having them repaired and upgraded by a construction crew that was supervised by a foreman, then selling them. I realized that if one of my construction foremen had screwed up as badly as I had, and as often as I had, I would have fired him. So, I wondered, *should I fire myself?*

At about that time, a friend gave me an audio copy of *The Power of Now* by Eckhart Tolle. I'd read it when it was first published in the late 1990s, so when I listened to it in audio format, I was already familiar with Eckhart Tolle and his ideas about getting free of the ego. Tolle's point, which he expresses in different ways in his books and online videos, is that all egos are ultimately dysfunctional.

It took me a while, but the more I listened to what Tolle had to say about the dysfunctional way all egos operate, the more I realized it applied to me. As I considered that, it seemed to me that in addition to being more conservative and better focused on present endeavors, I would be better off without an ego. But what is the ego, and how can a person get free of it? I turned to spiritual books, and to books on psychology, for an answer to the first part of that question. Here is what I found:

'Ego' is the Latin word for 'I.' Included in that definition is the single-core idea most people have that they're separate and apart from the rest of creation, plus the many related ideas people use to create within their own minds a unique personal identity.

In psychology, the word ego means *"The self; that which feels, acts, or thinks."* It is further defined to include a person's sense of self-worth and, more particularly, their sense of self-importance. And the separate ego-self I created as being me was indeed self-important. However, all of my importance was just a story in my head; in fact, the separate "I" that people carry around with them is *only* that and nothing else at all.

When people protect and defend their ego, they're supporting a story-in-their-head in which their ego-self is the main character. Their story can be good or bad, happy or sad, with lots of secondary characters and life events along the way, but the all-important main character never changes. That main character is, of course, the ego, and it has a lot of built-in protective systems.

If an enlightened psychologist were to have a conversation with someone's ego, it might go something like this:

Enlightened Psychologist

"The way the ego blocks and prevents people from fully awakening is by coloring their experience of life with an overlay of thoughts, stories, opinions, judgments, and ideas that obscure their ability to clearly see and understand things. Those obscuring thoughts, which might best be called mental noise, can also include dwelling on past events, anxiety or fear about a possible future event, the idea that they have been disrespected, thoughts about enemies they will never forgive, and more."

Ego Response

"Hey, I don't color or block anything. I see things as they are and how they are likely to turn out. That is an important part of my job!"

Enlightened Psychologist

"What those distracting thoughts have in common is either (a) the person thinking them believes they are or will be personally impacted by whatever their current mental noise is, or (b) those thoughts enhance the importance of the ego in the mind of its host, or (c) both. All such thoughts, which are, of course, just a story-in-the-head, act to take a person's attention away from the present moment, now. And now is the only time a person can be present, awake, and effective. Right now."

Ego Response

"I'm much more awake than you are, and what you call mental noise is actually me protecting you—me you're toast!"

Enlightened Psychologist

"The development of an ego is a natural part of the development of all children. The first vestiges of an ego appear in babies and very young children as they go through what child psychologists refer to as separation-individuation. The ego is then further developed through imaginary play in which young children can take on any number of different roles. When involved in such play, a child will often step fully into a role he or she is imagining, as though it is real, and their imaginary scenario can be so interesting to them that they may not immediately notice an adult who is trying to get their attention."

Ego Response

"That's irrelevant. My job is to look out for you, and I'm not a child. Let's move on!"

Enlightened Psychologist

"The ego becomes an important mental reference point for children as they continue to mature and learn to self-regulate. That is the term child psychologists use when talking about how children learn to control their behavior without the need for parental guidance. Psychologists tell us that egos in young people get further developed as they go through their teenage years. During those stages of development, they begin to compare themselves with others more frequently in order to see how they fit in with their peers."

Ego Response

"Finally, some common sense! Of course, I compare myself to others. That is how I know where I fit in. It is also how I discovered that, in many ways, I'm quite special!"

Enlightened Psychologist

"It is also during the teen years that young people may more frequently judge and condemn something or someone, or more frequently attack the ego of another person. They do that so as to inflate their own feelings of self-importance and personal autonomy. That strengthens their egoic idea that they are a separate and apart from others."

Ego Response

"Noticing how others mess up and telling people about it is certainly not an attack. It is one of the ways I help people. *Geeeeze.*"

Enlightened Psychologist

"A good metaphor for the ego-I that all children create might be the training wheels on a bicycle. It is what children naturally attach as an overlay onto their conscious, intelligent awareness while playing imaginary roles and while further refining those roles as they grow up. What happens with most people as they physically mature into adults is that those training wheels (the ego-I) remain attached and merge ever more deeply into a person's sense of being a separate self. That happens because they have become identified with stories-in-their-head about themselves; it is who they believe they are."

Ego Response

"Hey, I'm not a set of damn training wheels! And all of my past comes with me. It makes me who I am."

Enlightened Psychologist

"To mature into a fully awakened adult, a person must move past their ego-identity; they must be willing to let go of the idea that they know who they are based on stories-in-the-head. Doing that allows their true being, which is pristine conscious, intelligent awareness, to shine through and be revealed. It requires giving up the idea that they know how the world works or that they know anything at all with absolute certainty. *Zen Mind, Beginner's Mind,* an adage from Zen Buddhism, is another way of saying the same thing. A beginner's mind is fresh, very much alive, and quite present in this moment."

<u>Ego Response</u>

"Blah, blah, blah."

<u>Enlightened Psychologist</u>

"The primary concern every ego has is the maintenance of itself as a separate and important entity. And the bigger the ego, the more likely it is that its host will start talking or acting in ways designed to get attention so as to inflate feelings of self-importance. It pays to be patient and, within reasonable boundaries, accepting when that happens, just as one is patient with children who may at times push for attention. Children can usually be brought around to focus again on the conversation or task at hand after being acknowledged. And the same is often true for egos, which is not surprising, given that all egos are originally created by children."

<u>Ego Response</u>

"I said we're done here."

<u>Enlightened Psychologist</u>

"Eckhart Tolle says that people usually need to have experienced a deep failure in life before they will look deep within and discover who they are beyond name and form; before they will discover what Ramana Maharshi, a truly extraordinary spiritual teacher from India who died in 1950, called the Self. That deep failure can then lead to the voluntary release, or involuntary dissolution, of their fictional mind-made-me egoic identity. Their true being, which has always been there, can then more easily act through them."

Tolle is right about that last part, and I'm a good example; I had to fail deeply on many levels before I was willing to free myself from my own ego. But I did get here, and I will be forever grateful. My ego was incompetent when it came to creating a peaceful and balanced life for me, and it was absolutely fired. I was not sure how to enforce that decision, so I made up my own rules about how to do it, and it worked.

What I did was hold in mind on a consistent basis, including a focused half-hour daily meditation, the idea that my ego was not real and that Patrick is not real. I trusted spiritual teachers I'd been reading, such as Tolle and Ramana Maharshi, so instead of identifying myself as Patrick, I held in mind the understanding that I am pure, pristine conscious awareness. And I did one other thing.

Tolle also talks about Presence and the One Life; those are his names for what most people call God. I was not sure at the time if God was real or was instead just a fairy tale for gullible people. However, if God was real and interested, then God was welcome to take over my life and run it. And if not, my ego was still fired and let the chips fall where they may. And that, as it turned out, was enough; the rest seemed to follow naturally.

One day less than a year after I started on the practices that led to the dissolution of my ego, something in me, in my consciousness, shifted in a way that is profound. I call it realizing the Truth of Being. And it was not only my consciousness that shifted; my entire set of life circumstances also started to change so dramatically that it is hard to believe I was homeless, sleeping outside, and broke just a few years earlier.

Now I am again married, and my wife and I run spiritual retreats in our multi-million dollar home that overlooks the Pacific Ocean on Oregon's southern coast. For those interested, please visit CoastalCliffsRetreats.com

Thank you for joining me on this brief journey which has lasted a lifetime. God bless you.

My name is **Patrick Dague.**

In the eyes of the world, I'm a failed businessman who lost everything and then fully recovered when I made some very basic changes in my life. In fact, I more than recovered, so much so that it is hard to believe. But it is nonetheless true.

One of the main keys that led to such a major turnaround in my life was that, after researching the subject, I decided to fire my ego. And I followed through on that decision.

The other key part of my story is that although I did not really believe in God when my life fell apart, and I lost everything, I nonetheless decided that if God was real, He was welcome to be in charge of my life. And if God was not real, my ego was still fired.

And wow, what a powerful combination of decisions! In just a few short years, I went from being homeless and broke to owning a multi-million dollar home overlooking the Pacific Ocean on Oregon's southern coast. My wife and I use it to host spiritual retreats.

My goal now is to share with others the empowering changes that are possible when an ego-based identity is released and the pristine, conscious, intelligent awareness that is God takes over a person's life.

Thank you for allowing me to share part of my journey with you.

CHAPTER 22

SURRENDER AND EXHALE

THE POWER OF SAYING NO

Walid Aboulnaga

For most of my business career in client servicing, my job was to make sure clients were satisfied and always happy. I was a "yes" man.

During my personal healing journey, I realized exactly what I didn't want in life. It became evident more than ever what I would no longer stand for, and that was when I finally awoke my inner "no."

We tend to vividly remember moments that take our breath away. Whether they are perceived as positive or negative, they somehow become engraved in our minds and hearts.

I can easily recall such moments as if they happened yesterday, some so powerful it plays like a movie in my mind, others only the intense feelings and emotions I felt at the time. I have clear memories of beautiful ones and difficult ones, all of which I'm grateful for, even those most challenging ones, as they helped shape the man I am today.

For this chapter, I remember and want to share a few of the heavy ones, such as the call from my brother telling me that our father was on his death bed and that I needed to take the next flight home in hopes of saying goodbye. Or the time the neurosurgeon opposite me explained the results of the MRI done on my brain, informing me that treatment would involve the removal of a small piece of my skull as well as the freezing of several cranial nerves. I remember every detail of that meeting, how waves of panic and fear flooded my body, despair rippled through every thought as hope faded from view. Another pivotal moment was navigating the sudden closure of the company I was managing as a result of a massive corruption plot that had just been exposed. This happened just a few months after buying a new home and a brand-new car.

The constant state of fight and flight almost seemed to burn fear, sadness, and anger into my very cells. The intense shock aftershock pushed my nervous system to its limit; my organs seemed to twist inside me, causing me physical pain as a result of the emotional pain I endured. My very breathing during these tough times seemed to stop, emotions so overwhelming making it a challenge to accept life-giving oxygen into my body.

I reflect on these moments now, and many others now behind me, and all fill me with gratitude. Now just a chapter in the book of my life, each experience is a gift of learning, an opportunity to embrace the greatest version of myself, and each still in some way constantly shaping the future chapters of my story. After many years of deep inner work, extensive meditation, and dedicated breathwork practices, I have come far on my healing journey. I came to the realization that *breath* plays a major factor in how we feel, how we control our state of mind, our perceptions, and essentially how we control the outcome. It took me a long time to come to that realization, but I came to trust the timing of these moments in life as: the beauty truly lies in the journey more than the destination.

The story of my own transformation began as a result of excruciating pain, radiating from the top right side of my head to my eyebrow and through my jaw and teeth. As my busy daytime schedule with its distractions came to an end, I would have normally welcomed the evening of relaxation, but now I was greeted by the relentless throbbing pain. I would dread the approach of the night. My thoughts and awareness, now focused inward, were unable to navigate past the pain and enter into a deep sleep. I let stress rule my life, but at the time didn't even realize I was stressed; that state became so normal to me. I was digging myself deeper and deeper into pain without taking time to heal.

My shamanic journey started as a result of wanting to heal that pain naturally. At first, I looked into stress and anger management courses. In parallel to working on the mind and soul, I began focusing on my physical healing. I started detoxification programs which included juice fasts, water fasts, coffee enemas, and you name it; I did it. I attended a silent retreat (Vipassana) in search of answers and understanding buried deep in my subconscious. This eventually led me to experience different types of plant medicines such as Ayahuasca, Wachuma, and Peyote. The journey continued into meditation, yoga, breathwork, sound healing, energy work, and many types of healing modalities that, at the time, I had never heard of.

I met incredible practitioners along the way, crystal healers, pranic healers, and Bio Magnetic therapists. I connected with Reiki Masters and countless healers sharing their gifts and light with the world. If you had told me back then that I'd be burning my skin and placing frog poison to heal and purify my body or talked about spirit animals and lower worlds, I would have simply laughed.

But having experienced these amazing healing methods firsthand, having journeyed to places I once thought didn't exist, I wouldn't be here today sharing this gift with the world. I succeeded in healing myself with the grace of God, the support of my wife and family, and with the assistance of the many healers and wonderful souls encountered on my journey. I would no longer need surgery, my life drastically changed its course, and for all of it, I am grateful. I learned we are all Shamans (healers), and we have the ability to truly heal both physically and emotionally.

So, here I was, the "yes man." I said yes to every opportunity, constantly wanting to sign a new contract, renew an existing one, or expand another—yes, yes, yes—not knowing that by doing this, there was a big price to pay. The cost was time with my family, physical health, mental health, the health and well-being of my team, being in constant and sometimes overwhelming stress, and having to put up with rude and difficult clients because I wanted to keep the business relationship going. It seemed that everything was coming at me from every angle simultaneously: the clients, suppliers, and the partners.

Is it bad luck I landed upon such an unpleasant group of people? Am I in the wrong industry? What am I doing wrong? Or is it me?

Surely something was going my way as I was successful, the business was profitable and thriving, but at what cost? My health was the cost.

Then something happened. It probably wasn't the result of just this one day. It was the accumulation of my experiences thus far in search of a cure, a miraculous remedy to ease the pain. It was the result of my willingness to open myself to the universe, to receive answers, to centuries-old knowledge and wisdom I would've previously brushed aside as mystic superstitious nonsense. But because my heart was open and my mind was ready to break free of the life that created this situation, a magical breathwork experience would be the beginning of a new me. Something special happened during the session, something I cannot explain. I was filled with answers and insights, feeling them in the depth of my heart and my soul. I vowed to myself: *Moving forward, I will never work with anyone who doesn't appreciate me or my work.* Any company or person who undervalued the services my team and I provided or are simply horrible to work with, I committed to saying no to them.

Sometimes we know when no must be said, yet we don't speak our truth. The key reason is usually fear. It's fear of the unknown, fear of others, how others may react, or fear of possible repercussions resulting from our authentic no. After months of self-discovery, I returned back home with a crystal-clear vision, and the first thing I did was say "no" to unfulfilling jobs or business opportunities from our clients. I embodied my newfound inner strength, and in honor of living my authentic truth, I terminated the company agreements with our long-standing key client of ten years.

They were our main source of revenue, our biggest client, and important to the survival of the business. Ending that toxic partnership felt liberating. My colleagues and friends were confused and dismayed, "How could you just let go of something that's making money so easily like that?" However, there was no doubt in my mind and heart that this was an essential element of my healing.

Separating from such a long-term partnership isn't that easy. Meeting after meeting took place in the weeks that followed the termination, and I managed to firmly keep saying no to all requests that I would have said yes to in the past.

Part of me wondered if another client would appear, filling the space the old had left. I wanted to attract a different type of client, where there was mutual respect and a collaborative approach to business, without the constant wave of corruption to avoid. In my mind, this would offer me a life of minimal stress and the financial freedom to continue life as before.

I waited patiently in the hopes that business would pick up again, but it didn't. A new chapter began and guided me gradually away from the corporate world; that was all I knew.

It was at this point I came to the awareness that to accept, welcome, and surrender to our future—to shout "yes" to our destiny from every fragment of our being—we must first hear our "no."

Many of us shy away from the concept of death. Birth is such a joyous celebration, but in this modern age, death is filled with loss and sorrow. Ancient cultures such as Bali still hold the beautiful tradition of celebrating and honoring the souls who've passed from this life. I look back now with joy at these turbulent times and view my no as a mini death of sorts, a path I walked my whole life that ended at the precise point it was meant to, in exactly the right way, and all to allow for the birth of a new path.

I gave myself permission, and I invite you to do the same, to say no to anything that will drain your energy or make you unhappy. Say no, even if it feels uncomfortable. Train yourself to say no without having to explain yourself; sometimes, no excuses are needed. I've learned the hard way that saying no is easy, it just needs some practice, and you'll wake up your own inner no. Just make sure you say no at the right time and for the right reasons, so you make every single yes count.

Learning to say no eventually led me to close the company I set up from scratch, a company I watched grow from inception to my own little empire, with a team of 1,400 employees covering 14 different countries across the Middle East and North Africa. I signed its first contract and its last. I created a successful business because of years of hard work and thousands of hours of dedication, yet on the day we closed shop, an unexpected sigh of relief followed, and I felt lighter as if a huge weight was lifted from my shoulders.

During Neuro-Linguistic Programming (NLP) training, we were taught to symbolically cut the umbilical cord that links you with trauma, with certain instances and precise moments you're holding on to. Although I didn't perceive the running of my company and its closure as traumatic, I now understand the profound effect it had on my physical, mental, and emotional health. By cutting the cord, I released it and let it go.

It was time for real change. After 20 years in business marketing and digital media, I entered the world of healing, travel, and adventure, something my spirit had yearned for all my life. Setting up NAFAS Journeys was once a dream, a vision during breathwork that turned into reality. After years of research, training, reading, and practicing, I set my goals and was determined to be in service, to help others heal, transform, and awaken their true potential as I have. I wanted to share my experience and knowledge and make NAFAS Journeys a success, not only financially but spiritually, touching the hearts of all those who join our journeys. Not only did I redirect the course of my career, but I also relocated my family to the magical island of Bali after living in Dubai for the previous 15 years. When you're too comfortable, you don't take risks, and you don't welcome change. Surely the pain in my head was a wake-up call, a gift to ignite a passion for life I hadn't thought was possible.

That very first breathwork gave me insights into what I would no longer tolerate and also opened me to what was next. I breathed during the session as I'd never breathed before. The feeling of energy in between my hands and throughout my body was immense. My body shook as energy circulated and pulsed through me. Light and heat filled my body with such intensity I felt like the sun. I felt a deep sense of oneness, connection, and love for everything and everyone; tears of pure joy flowed in gratitude, for that moment, for every moment that life had given me and would give me. I felt the pieces of my life finally taking form and connecting. The name **NAFAS** came to me during this breathwork. Not only that but the image of the logo as well. *Nafas* means (Breath) in Arabic and is derived from the word *Nafs,* which translates to (Spirit/Self), and breath and Spirit are the same word in many languages.

Not only did I gain insights into what would soon be my new company's name and logo, but I even future traveled during the breathwork and envisioned myself hosting our first retreat, which we now call *Soulventures,* adventures for the Soul. I could see myself with our tribe on the last day of the program. I could feel the gratitude and happiness from those who would join vibrate from the future. I was feeling the healing that took place, and I could feel the love and appreciation from the tribe for the experience I created for them.

Following the breathing session, I quickly took note of all I saw, felt, and received. From that point, everything seemed to flow effortlessly, from the formation of the company with its name (now a true reflection of my vision) to the first Soulventure, which took place in Ubud, Bali, in November 2018. Following my shamanic training, I was able to facilitate breathwork experiences, giving others the opportunity to connect to their inner wisdom, receive answers and guidance, and heal. I helped people learn to trust in their path and understand that they are always guided in every step as part of the journey. This, too, like the ability to say no comfortably and more often, took time for me to grasp. I look back at the first journey and how I worried about and tried to control every small detail.

My mind put a negative spin on every moment. The familiar stress response I hadn't felt for so long was present, but now I was armed with the tools to deal with it. I was able to observe the situation, acknowledge the fear and anxiety, then enter into meditation, where I visualized and felt the success of the entire journey from beginning to end. This process allows me to connect and manifest an outcome on the physical, emotional, and energetic levels. The most powerful tool we have in this process is used when emotionally we live the outcome through feelings. The stronger the emotions attached to the visualization, the more we attract our desires.

During the meditation prior to the event, I felt a message that came to me: *I will shine for you.* I smiled. Mama Bali was letting me know all would be fine. I finally surrendered to the outcome of that day and each day after. The sun shone for the hike and reminded me to trust my inner voice. My vision during my first breathwork came to life, and I could feel the gratitude and love from those who were present, just as I did during the breathwork.

The success of that first Soulventure and the life-changing experiences I witnessed in those who joined led me to expand my vision further.

I share my story for all those who are struggling to find their next step in life, for those looking for peace of mind and a serene perspective on life. If you're feeling stressed, anxious, have panic attacks, or are going through a difficult time, whether it be a physical or emotional injury, loss of a loved one, death, losing a job, business or investments, it's not an easy situation to be in. Whatever state you may be feeling, I invite you to come back to the breath. Allow the breath to be your guide, measuring how you feel. Taking slow deep breaths while you're calm and relaxed, consciously aware of the inhale and the exhale, will help you be relaxed and focused in times of stress or any tense moment.

The famous 13th century Sufi poet Rumi once wrote, "Yesterday I was clever, so I wanted to change the world. Today I am wise, so I am changing myself."

I've learned to say no, trust and surrender, and now I always remember to breathe when things get out of hand. This is an open invitation to take a deep NAFAS with me, for life is beautiful, and with a good deep breath, you can learn to experience it like never before.

Walid Aboulnaga co-founded, managed, and ran multiple successful businesses in the Middle East and North Africa with a team of over 1,400 members from 14 different countries. After witnessing and experiencing firsthand the destructive effects of stress, he sensed a need for a deeper connection with our true potential and awareness of our mind, body, and Spirit. As a result, *NAFAS Journeys* was launched in 2018, a Transformational Travel Experience helping those embarking on their lifelong journey and quest for self-discovery by bridging adventure with spirituality.

He has trained with some of the most knowledgeable and experienced breath masters, including Shamanic Breathwork under Venus Rising, Stanislov Grof's Holotropic Breathwork, the Wim Hof Method, Breath Mastery with Dan Brule, and many more. Walid is a certified Shamanic Breathwork Facilitator and Ordained a Shamanic Minister. He was also a member of the Entrepreneur's Organization (EO) for the last ten years. He currently lives in Bali with his wife Katrina and three daughters, Luna, Skye, and Theia.

Bringing in his experience from the multiple different techniques of breathwork, he has led thousands of people across different countries between his breathwork workshops and transformational retreats. An adventurer committed to helping others see their true potential and experience deep transformation through bringing breath awareness and conscious breathing into everyday practices.

Learn to say "no" to the good, so you can say "yes" to the best.

~Walid Aboulnaga, Founder NAFAS Journeys

walid@nafas.life

www.nafas.life

@nafasjourneys

MEDITATION TO BALANCE THE DIVINE FEMININE AND MASCULINE ENERGIES

Close your eyes and breathe in and breathe out. Envision yourself surrounded by blue Christ light, kept by the Pleiadians, that transmutes all negative emotions.

Breathe it in, letting the blue light fill every cell of your body—acknowledging each and every cell. Breathe out, exhaling all the way down to the core of Mother Earth. Ask her to hold you tightly, grounding you all the way to the Crystalline Grid.

Pull up clean, pure energy from Mother Earth through each of the chakras, connecting all the way from Gaia up to Helios, the Great Central Sun, and Source.

Call yourself back to yourself across all time, space, universes, lifetimes, dimensions, and incarnations, past, present and future.

Then call yourself down to yourself into your heart space, so you may live and manifest as one, sovereign over self.

Breathe in the blue light again. Feel the expansiveness of the blue light, growing bigger and bigger and bigger. At this time, call in the Light Blue Violet Pleiadian Dragons.

Starting with the Earth Star Chakra, breathe in the blue Christ Light to balance, rotate, centre, and calibrate this chakra, and remove all that does not serve. May the light blue violet Pleiadian Dragon energy balance the Divine Feminine and the Divine Masculine energy, past, present and future, and please clear, release and entrap any non-resonant energy and replace it all with unconditional love.

Move to the Root Chakra, breathe in the blue Christ Light to balance, rotate, centre, and calibrate this chakra, and remove all that does not serve. May the light blue violet Pleiadian Dragon energy balance the Divine Feminine and the Divine Masculine energy, past, present and future, and please clear, release and entrap any non-resonant energy and replace it all with unconditional love.

Move to the Sacral Chakra, breathe in the blue Christ Light to balance, rotate, centre, and calibrate this chakra, and remove all that does not serve. May the light blue violet Pleiadian Dragon energy balance the Divine Feminine and the Divine Masculine energy, past, present and future, and please clear, release and entrap any non-resonant energy and replace it all with unconditional love.

Move to the Naval Chakra, breathe in the blue Christ Light to balance, rotate, centre, and calibrate this chakra, and remove all that does not serve. May the light blue violet Pleiadian Dragon energy balance the Divine Feminine and the Divine Masculine energy, past, present and future, and please clear, release and entrap any non-resonant energy and replace it all with unconditional love.

Move to the Solar Plexus Chakra, breathe in the blue Christ Light to balance, rotate, centre, and calibrate this chakra, and remove all that does not serve. May the light blue violet Pleiadian Dragon energy balance the Divine Feminine and the Divine Masculine energy, past, present and future, and please clear, release and entrap any non-resonant energy and replace it all with unconditional love.

Move to the Heart Chakra, breathe in the blue Christ Light to balance, rotate, centre, and calibrate this chakra, and remove all that does not serve. May the light blue violet Pleiadian Dragon energy balance the Divine Feminine and the Divine Masculine energy, past, present and future, and please clear, release and entrap any non-resonant energy and replace it all with unconditional love.

Move to the High Heart Chakra, breathe in the blue Christ Light to balance, rotate, centre, and calibrate this chakra, and remove all that does not serve. May the light blue violet Pleiadian Dragon energy balance the Divine Feminine and the Divine Masculine energy, past, present and future, and please clear, release and entrap any non-resonant energy and replace it all with unconditional love.

Move to the Throat Chakra, breathe in the blue Christ Light to balance, rotate, centre, and calibrate this chakra, and remove all that does not serve. May the light blue violet Pleiadian Dragon energy balance the Divine Feminine and the Divine Masculine energy, past, present and future, and please clear, release and entrap any non-resonant energy and replace it all with unconditional love.

Move to the Third Eye Chakra, breathe in the blue Christ Light to balance, rotate, centre, and calibrate this chakra, and remove all that does not serve. May the light blue violet Pleiadian Dragon energy balance the Divine Feminine and the Divine Masculine energy, past, present and future, and please clear, release and entrap any non-resonant energy and replace it all with unconditional love.

Move to the Crown Chakra, breathe in the blue Christ Light to balance, rotate, centre, and calibrate this chakra, and remove all that does not serve. May the light blue violet Pleiadian Dragon energy balance the Divine Feminine and the Divine Masculine energy, past, present and future, and please clear, release and entrap any non-resonant energy and replace it all with unconditional love.

Move to the Causal Chakra, breathe in the blue Christ Light to balance, rotate, centre, and calibrate this chakra, and remove all that does not serve. May the light blue violet Pleiadian Dragon energy balance the Divine Feminine and the Divine Masculine energy, past, present and future, and please clear, release and entrap any non-resonant energy and replace it all with unconditional love.

Move to the Solar Star Chakra, breathe in the blue Christ Light to balance, rotate, centre, and calibrate this chakra, and remove all that does not serve. May the light blue violet Pleiadian Dragon energy balance the Divine Feminine and the Divine Masculine energy, past, present and future, and please clear, release and entrap any non-resonant energy and replace it all with unconditional love.

Moving to the Stellar Gateway Chakra, breathe in the blue Christ Light to balance, rotate, centre, and calibrate this chakra, and remove all that does not serve. May the light blue violet Pleiadian Dragon energy balance the Divine Feminine and the Divine Masculine energy, past, present and future, and please clear, release and entrap any non-resonant energy and replace it all with unconditional love.

Now, ask the Dragons to hand off all non-resonant energies that have been entrapped to the Unicorns to be taken to Helios to be transmuted.

Thank the Unicorns, thank the Dragons.

Breathe in blue Christ Light, pull it down through all your chakras and exhale asking Gaia to ground you in this moment of balance. Pull pure energy up from Mother Earth to the heart space, extend your arms to freely share unconditional love in balanced Divine Feminine and Divine Masculine energy for the best and highest good of all.

And so it is, and so it is, and so it shall be.

Namaste.

Channeled for Dianna Leeder

By Maysha www.AkasaLiving.net

A LAST MESSAGE
TO READERS

Thank you for reading this book and allowing us to share the journeys of transcendent men with you. You being here is a hand outstretched to each of our authors in recognition of the lived experiences and healing they've done that's invited them to share their personal stories for those who need to read them.

I love the integration of the energies of the Divine Masculine and Diving Feminine in each of us. We are whole beings called to express and be that oneness that is only accessible when we recognize all of who we are. We are not just men or women, energetically we are both.

Honouring that integration redefines masculinity, even from a purely gender perspective, by recognizing who we authentically are. My partner in this book, R Scott Holmes, makes reference to "How to be a guy without being an asshole". I appreciate that. After all, men (or women) who determine their authentic selves rarely find "being an asshole" on the list.

We do this work for ourselves, but truthfully we do it for everyone. We are no longer separate from our authentic selves, allowing us to reduce the gaps that exist among us. Individually, we support, love and hold space for those who need it. A healthier world and planet rises from there.

I hope you've found goodness in something you've read here. There is always more to experience and living a transcendent life is yet another way to support, and be supported to live from the heart. There may be shadows in your way, but there are many opportunities to dance with them, right here on these pages.

Transcendence isn't just a concept, it's a way of life that keeps us strong and connected to ourselves, our humanity and to those around us. It's something to be celebrated, and I am eager to hear your journey. You may find a bump or two along the way, but you'll being guided by your wholeness and your higher self.

Please, review this book on Amazon and share with friends. You will help us give other men the awareness to investigate, embrace, and walk the path of transcendence too.

Dianna xo

WHOLE-HEARTED THANKS

I begin with R Scott Holmes. You brought me this project, leaving it wide open for me to support your goal of promoting men's transcendence in whatever way I designed, giving me room to be myself as well as honour the Find Your Voice, Save Your Life book series. Throughout the entire project, you showed up fully in support of the authors, knowing that transcendent men need to be celebrated. You have that "guy" connection that for a time I wondered if I could replicate, but you very soon showed me that I didn't need to. And you showed up for me with each meeting or phone call, as a real transcended man in action; doing your own healing work to display both your Diving Feminine and your Divine Masculine traits, never wavering from your heart space, never letting your energy reduce to a dense vibration. From the community building that you held your hand out to, to your deep appreciation and respect for me and my role as a woman leading a book for men, you gave me reason to call you friend. Getting to know you through the Find Your Voice Healer Certification training didn't hurt either! You are an incredible gift to this book, Scott, and to the work of becoming a transcendent man. The part of your inner self behind the mission of finding and using our voices as men and women is strong, powerful and show you walking the talk. Thank you seems feeble, but know it comes from my heart. You are and will continue to be a champion for finding your voice, transcendence, and someone that will always be a friend. With gratitude, appreciation, deep respect and love.

Readers, we are grateful for you. You're the reason we're here. As we read books like this, we bring ourselves to the pages and look for what resonates, what we can take away as gifts from the read. We are honoured if you find even one thing that changes your perspective and supports you to live closer to your authentic self, you'll be supporting others to do the same in the process. Thank you for being here, being open, and helping another man find his transcendent voice. We could not get to my goal of empowering every single human to use their voice more and live out loud without you!

Authors, how do Scott and I thank you? We read your stories and our hearts blossomed open a little more with each one, yet we recognized that your pain, your transition, your transformation was so much more for you than what you could put in your story. Yet here you are, offering yourself so another man can heal. To say we have deep love, respect and appreciation for each of you is an understatement. You have joined our mission to change the world, one transcendent man using his voice at a time. In this community you are now forever a part of, we've consistently witnessed the love, respect and the holding of space for people and relationships. No surprise there, that's who you are. That is what transcendence has meant to you. We are forever indebted and are proud to be a tiny part of your world, connected by these pages and the work we do in service to others.

Laura DiFranco, I once described you as the badass of badasses and I'm sticking to that. Scott would agree that you are not just a publisher, you connect with each author from a genuine place of love, respect and a desire to help them help others. Pure, honest, and quite transcendent of you! I will say again that I see you as a soul sister on this path of helping men and women find their voices, we have a partnership that continues to be strong and resilient. You have helped me strengthen my voice in ways I never expected, helping me reach my personal authenticity but also reach those who my purpose directs me to serve. From there I can offer my goodness from the same place you offer yours…your heart. Thank you. I am incredibly grateful for who you are, what you do, and that you joined me on this journey.

Dino Marino, deep thanks for a job well done as our book designer for Find Your Voice, Save Your Life 4. You held space for us until we got it just right, being experienced enough to know that we needed to love all of it, and we do. We are grateful.

Guy Kilchrist, you have not just contributed as an author for this book, but also given us the most amazing image for our front cover. Your art is expressive and honours the journey of a transcended man who needs to meet his shadow, clear to you because you have embraced the rise of transcendence in yourself. We are honoured to share your artistic, heart felt abilities with the world through this book. We hope the world sees the talent that you hold, it is immense. Thank you.

Family and friends, those who give us space to do this work, you are so appreciated. Both Scott and I are grateful for you, especially Glen and Patti who had family time with us interrupted by calls and meetings. We love you and your support of what you know we need to do to fulfill our purpose in this world. We are so grateful to have your backing on this journey, it would never be as easy without it. Special shout out to my daughters Paige and Whitney, their life partners, and my amazing little grandchildren. If this work supports any of you to get closer to your best self, living from the heart, it's all worth it. Thank you for loving as you do, your support means everything.

Launch team. You rocked it! You didn't just step up, you jumped in with both feet and helped us get this book out to the world with your encouragement and praise for our efforts. You are an integral part of our team and we truly could not have done this without you! You have upwardly moved the bar for transcendence. Take some time to hear and feel our gratitude. Thank you, thank you, thank you!

ABOUT DIANNA LEEDER

Dianna Leeder is a Canadian author, podcaster, and owner of Crave More Life Coaching. She is a Certified Professional Co-Active Coach, and an American Confidence Institute Certified Confidence Coach.

She has dedicated the last four decades to helping people find and use their voices, intuitively seeing their blocks to being authentic to themselves and holding the space of self-understanding, self-acceptance and unconditional love. Dianna opens them up to being themselves and having the relationship experiences they truly want, need, and desire.

Her own path of un-silencing herself has become the journey through which she coaches others and certifies Find Your Voice Healers. She holds the power of each of us to heal and live our purpose by aligning to self as sacred and honourable. From clients to her own grand babes, Dianna's message is simple.

"Look inside."

She believes the time of living with silenced voices is over and offers clients a journey of self-exploration to find and use their voices, a platform for healing through writing both published and unpublished works, and the Find Your Voice Healers Certification Training for coaches and healers.

Dianna lives in the Toronto, Canada area and shares her life with her hubby, two daughters and their partners, her three super fun grandkids that she intentionally creates her relationships with, and her future dog. She's into travel, designing aligned space, and the healing of the planet.

Learn more about Dianna, her coaching programs and how to become a Certified Find Your Voice Healer at:

https://cravemorelife.com

Follow Dianna on Social

https://www.facebook.com/CraveMoreLife/

https://twitter.com/cravemorelife
https://www.instagram.com/diannaleeder/
https://www.pinterest.ca/cravemorelife
For resources and bonus gifts from Dianna, go to:
https://cravemorelife.com/findyourvoice

Join Dianna's free Facebook group Find Your Voice Women
www.facebook.com/groups/findyourvoicewomen
Join Scott's' free Facebook group Find Your Voice, Transcendent Men
https://www.facebook.com/groups/findyourvoicemen

To hire Dianna or Scott to speak to your group
FINDING YOUR VOICE AND HOW TO GET THERE
contact Dianna at:
dianna@cravemorelife.com